TESSERAE

A mosaic of poems by Zimbabwean women

Compiled and edited by
Samantha Rumbidzai Vazhure and Marian Christie

Carnelian Heart Publishing

First published in Great Britain in 2023 by:

Carnelian Heart Publishing Ltd
Suite A
82 James Carter Road
Mildenhall
Suffolk
IP28 7DE
UK

www.carnelianheartpublishing.co.uk

©Each individual poem, the contributing poet
©This anthology as a collective work, Carnelian Heart Publishing Ltd 2023

Paperback ISBN   978-1-914287-46-6
Hardback   978-1-914287-47-3
Ebook ISBN   978-1-914287-48-0

A catalogue record for this book is available from the British Library.

All rights reserved. No part of this publication may be reproduced, stored in a retrieval system or transmitted in any form or by any means, electronic, mechanical, photocopying, recording or otherwise without prior written permission from the publisher.

Compiled and Edited by:
Samantha Rumbidzai Vazhure & Marian Christie

Cover art:
Lin Barrie

Cover layout:
Carnelian Heart Publishing and Rebeca Covers

Internal design:
Typeset by Carnelian Heart Publishing Ltd
Layout and formatting by DanTs Media

Taking flight, winged woman, freedom is a state of mind

Take flight, winged woman,
lift your head and your hands to the heavens.
Close your thoughts....

Criticism and abuse are physical constraints,
but freedom is a state of mind.

Lin Barrie

Introduction

Twenty-five years ago, Zimbabwean women made literary history by publishing *three* anthologies dedicated to poetry. The Zimbabwe Women Writers association was building on its legacy of mutual support for women authors by highlighting a marginalized genre, poetry. Founded in 1990, ZWW has encouraged writers of all genres since its inaugural anthology edited by Norma Kitson in 1994. But the year of 1998 was special in its celebration of writing in multiple national languages: *Inkondlo* in Ndebele; *Nhetembo* in Shona and *Poetry and Short Stories* in English offered evidence of how much poetry appealed to women writers, and how it had the potential to create a community of readers as well as poets. While *Tesserae* was conceived of and completed independently of ZWW, the foundations for the poetry in this anthology are deep and it is only by understanding our poetic lineage that we can fully recognize innovation.

Poetry in the vernacular languages of Zimbabwe is interwoven into the most fundamental aspects of identity, with snippets of clan poetry seasoning many of our greetings. For many, hymns and ceremonial music place poetry at the core of spiritual expression, while some of our most beloved musicians are masters of lyric poetry, whether sung or, in cases like Hope Masike's, also written. From the earliest days of published Zimbabwean literature, poetry has occupied a significant role, and each anthology presents a snapshot of the national psyche and artistry in all its rich variations. Yet it is painfully obvious that the first poetry collections published after independence severely underestimated women's creativity. The first anthology to challenge this was Flora Veit-Wild's *Patterns of Poetry in Zimbabwe* in 1988. Devoting a full chapter to each of seven poets, she presented the most significant cluster of poems by a Zimbabwean woman, Kristina Rungano, in the anthology. Like the ZWW collections a decade later, *Patterns* shows us the power of anthologies for making women visible, and placing their writing in context. The leading role of women like Irene Staunton and Jane Morris at publishing houses like Baobab Books, Weaver Press, and ama'Books is another factor in our literary history, and it is gratifying to see how Carnelian Heart Press, Samantha Vazhure's UK-based publishing venture, is extending this dynamic across the diaspora. All of these precedents were harbingers of the rich development of women's poetry whose most recent fruits are presented in the collection here in your hands.

Tesserae represents a significant moment in the history of Zimbabwean women's writing, for it is the first collection published by a Zimbabwean woman-*owned* press, independently edited, and entirely composed of women's poetry. The creative influences for the contributors to this volume reflect generational changes. For some, the legacy of our national literary elders resonates – the bold claims to the power of the pen in Freedom Nyamubaya's poetry, or the poetic prose of Yvonne Vera, for example. Others reflect more recent influences, particularly spoken word. But throughout, the voices here are also wholly original, and one of the best aspects of the collection is how it offers a sample of more than one poem by each author represented. Taking its name from the individual tiles that make up a mosaic, the title is in the plural – meaning it is not just one tile, but several in each of the colours of these poets' imaginations that make up a formidable whole. The co-editors, Samantha Vazhure and Marian Christie, present a diverse display of women's creativity, drawing from multiple generations, styles, themes, and heritages. The process of assembling the collection is a fascinating story of its own, and even the title's symbolism is poetic. Gathering these poems began with an invitation sent as far and wide as possible, asking Zimbabwean women to contribute to "Project Venus," a new anthology. This is not an encyclopaedic volume so much as a welcoming reception for those who chose to submit work. As Samantha Vazhure tells it,

> "Long before the title was decided, I instinctively named the project Venus, for obvious reasons. Venus, the planet is associated with femininity. Venus, the mythological Greek goddess encompasses beauty, desire, sex, fertility, love, prosperity and victory."

When the poems had been selected, the title emerged organically. Here is Vazhure, again, in her own words:

> "The word 'tesserae' came to mind because mosaic craft is a concept I'm familiar with, as a visual artist. Marian, as a mathematician is also intimate with the concept of tessellations, so when she came on board as editor, she loved that idea. When the time came to decide the title of the anthology, we wanted a title that embodied the properties of 'Venus' as well as the diversity of poets contributing to the anthology."

This beautifully conceived title was also deeply anchored in space, place, and geography, for the editors note that Tesserae are regions with the oldest material on the most deformed terrains on the surface of planet Venus. And what makes this particularly apt for Zimbabwe is that a 'Tessera' is also a small piece of stone, glass, or ceramic used in the craft or construction of mosaics. The iconic Great Zimbabwe Monument, 'the house of stone', is a mosaic in its own right, and the editors felt that "the voices in this anthology are 'tesserae' crafting the panorama of Zimbabwean womanhood."

One of the most tiresome questions African writers are asked is *who is the audience?* So let us begin with the first readers – the other poets in the collection. This anthology allows writers who may never encounter each other in person to discover each other's voices and develop a deeper understanding of our vision, struggles, common interests, and individual quirks. It is only in gatherings such as this that one can speak of *Zimbabwean women writers* as a collective, occasions where we can develop a knowledge of each other's work that will stimulate mutual references and an exchange of ideas on theme, form, and purpose. The decision to organize this anthology alphabetically *by first name* is the first step in our making friends. For the handful of writers who have published full-length collections, this anthology solves a perennial problem, the difficulty of distributing books published elsewhere. It may be that obtaining full-length books like Tariro Ndoro's *Agringada: Like a Gringa, Like a Foreigner* published by Mojaji in South Africa, or the chapbooks by Charity Hutete-Makawa and Blessing Musariri, published by the African Poetry Book Fund in the U.S. is unfeasible. But this anthology will enable all of the writers included to circulate a sample of their work more easily within and beyond Zimbabwe. Who knows how many writers will be "discovered" by readers drawn by more general interest, given how diverse and distinctive each of the poets here is. It is our hope that budding writers and lovers of culture faced with the challenging conditions of life in Zimbabwe will see a reflection of the immense creative energies that remain our most inexhaustible natural resource. The collection is also for those working for the rights of women, girls, femmes, and non-binary individuals. Several poets bravely bare their experiences of gendered oppression, but it is also evident even in the more subtle investigations into emotional and domestic labour, a quest for autonomy and privacy, and also the vitality and strategies for survival reflected here. Each voice is proof that the arts belong at the centre of our being, lending nuanced, visceral insights into dilemmas that cannot be solved by statistics or algorithms alone. As a whole, *Tesserae* will also become a tile in the growing mosaic of contemporary African poetry. The audience for such work is clear in the rise of several Africa-specific poetry competitions, dedicated publishing initiatives, and flourishing online communities. It is also apparent in the fact that more and more educators and researchers are taking up African poetry. But ultimately, the audience for this collection is you, reader, you who have come with a curious mind to see how each of these poets makes our world anew.

And what will you find in this mosaic? Let me overwhelm you with glimpses of these tiles. Assembling them as you read at your own pace will be your way to join the creative process:… a traveller's longing for home… tender memories of a miscarried child… a whirlwind whipping a coming of age story into a metaphor in a mere four lines…the rhythm of childhood games… embracing one's own contradictions… lines stretched across a whole page evoking an angel's wingspan… a marriage maturing into the hectic pace of family life… the unconditional love of a mother-in-law, "everything I expected, and didn't"… laments for countrymen at risk of xenophobia… the beauty of our landscape reflected in a sister's tribute… erotic confidence in the embrace of another woman… determination to "give birth to myself/every time I refuse/ to let them annihilate my spirit"… a stern warning of how our house of stone, once a mansion of dreams, sometimes seems to be masquerading as ruins… a father's elegy resonating with the best oral traditions… empathy for the jobless… Read on, and discover the new patterns of poetry among Zimbabwean women.

Tsitsi Jaji, Durham, NC, July 2023

Editors' Note

Zimbabwe has a rich creative tradition, with a wealth of poetic talent. However, opportunities and exposure are limited, particularly for contemporary Zimbabwean women poets. As editors we have sought to address this. From the outset our aims were clear: we wanted to provide a safe space in which Zimbabwean women could express themselves through poetry; to include a broad representation of voices, backgrounds, and experiences; and to make a statement about the cultural importance of poetry, its value in resisting oppressive forces, in acknowledging the power of history, memories and traditions, in sharing perspectives and seeking catharsis.

Tesserae is a unique celebration of Zimbabwean womanhood in all its diversity, its richness of voice and theme and narrative. The contributors include traditional page poets and underground poets, students and grandmothers, visual poets and spoken word artists, established writers and emerging talents, from within Zimbabwe and from the diaspora. In their poetry they explore wide-ranging themes, including challenging or traditionally taboo subjects. Domestic abuse, xenophobia, queerness, illicit relationships, sexual fantasy, menstruation, and suicidal ideation all feature within these pages. There are tender portrayals of family, friendships and parenthood; narratives of loss and despair; humorous poems; socio-political commentaries; transcendent allegories and lyrical descriptions, inter-woven with pulsing natural energy. Scents, sounds, tastes and visual images of Zimbabwe form an ever-present backdrop, at times overtly, at times indirectly. Voices resonate in vibrant harmony; poems engage each other in subliminal conversation.

In her essay *Disobedient Poetics – Translating the Third Space*, Tariro Ndoro reflects eloquently on how language and our sense of identity are intertwined. Language is the instrument of poetry. As such it is many-layered, its music weaving internalised rhythms and cadences of the culture, oral traditions, memories and experiences that have formed us. It is surely no coincidence that several poems in this anthology touch on the complex relationship between language, identity, and 'home'.

Compiling, editing, and preparing *Tesserae* for publication has been an immensely rewarding experience. We extend our thanks to all the contributors, who have trusted us with their beautiful poems and with whom it has been a joy and a privilege to work. We are grateful to Lin Barrie for her inspirational cover art; Tsitsi Ella Jaji for her insightful Introduction; and Tariro Ndoro for her cogent essay on poetics. Our wish is that you, the reader, will enjoy this intricately patterned mosaic of poetry, with its subtle complementarities and vivid contrasts. Each voice is powerful and distinctive. Each poet has her own unique story to tell.

Samantha Rumbidzai Vazhure and Marian Christie

Contents

Introduction — vii
Editors' Note — xi

Afric McGlinchey — 21
Birthstone — 22
In my dreams I travel home to Africa… — 23
Last Conquest — 24
White Sky — 25
On the soles of their feet — 26
Eighteen — 28

Ashleigh Mafemba — 29
Two-faced — 30
Speaking in Tongues — 31
They don't write about us — 32
Hymn of Rebirth — 34

Carla-Ann Makumbe — 35
My tales — 36
Delirium — 37
Chaos Reincarnated — 38
To the angel who watches over me — 39

Charity Hutete-Makawa — 40
How to birth an adult — 41
Converted — 42
The Art of Smiling — 43
And then it's not — 44
Love's Extras — 45

Chioniso Tsikisayi — 46
Exchange Rate — 47
The Next Great Baker — 48
HardTalk — 49
Thunderstorms and Hibiscus Leaves — 50

I Want to Fall Apart Quietly											51
Planting is a Heavy Thing											52

Cristol Danai Mubaiwa											**53**
No Byes My Love											54
Period											55
Behind The Curtains											56
Mhamha											58

Cynthia Rumbidzai Marangwanda											**60**
Birth											61
Echoes											62
Stone Mansion											63
Remembrance											64
Sista Outsiders											66
Loud											68

Deborah Nyasha Kabongo											**69**
The Dancer and the Filmmaker (Cumcorder)											70
Secrets the Garbage Man Knew (Madhodhabhini)											71
Photograph											72

Ethel Irene Kabwato											**73**
In Remembrance											74
Mothers and Babies											75
Mother of the Revolution											76
For Creedence											78
Whispers in the Dark											80
Africa Day											84

Fikile Sithembiso Mkandla											**86**
Kuvelaphi?											87
Kum'nyama lapha!											88
Escape											89

Fungai Rufaro Machirori											**90**
Re-entry											91
The Imposition											92

Night Harvesters — 94
undone — 95
KFC on a Friday Night — 96
Seven — 97

Gertrude Mutsamwira — **98**
Lost Love — 99
Joblessness — 100
Absent in Your Presence — 102

Josephine Muganiwa — **103**
The Golden Handcuffs — 104
Cruelty — 105
Shades of sleep — 106
Paintings — 107

Kimberly Mhlanga — **108**
Pieces of Us — 109
Dearest Mother — 110
Affliction! — 111
A Cry for Help — 112

Lin Barrie — **113**
Embrace Equity — 114
Portrait, taking flight — 116
A kite with a broken string has all the sky — 118
Water — 120
Fire — 122

Lucille Sambo — **124**
Wait in the sun — 125
R(restricted) — 126
Waning Gibbous — 128
Fog — 130
Mistle thrush — 133

Marian Christie — **134**
Turbulence — 135

Daffodils — 136
lines — 137
Citizen of nowhere — 138
Because no matter how hard I try, I don't understand the rules — 139
And for the rest of time — 140

Mercy Dhliwayo — **141**
Cycles — 142
Dear Black Man — 143
Childhood Paintings — 144
The Weight of our Fathers' Names — 145
Jacaranda — 146

Nyasha Celeste Makombe — **148**
I write — 149
Lend me a rope — 150
Mirror — 152
Should I return — 153

Nyasha Norah Mavhu — **154**
Diluted — 155
The Cursed One — 156
Long Gone — 157
The Greed in Me — 158

Patience Tinotenda Mutsetse — **159**
How Our Fathers Break Our Hearts — 160
Silencing my Voice — 161
Buried Deep Within Us — 162
Behind — 163
I Have a Habit — 164

Pauline Chirata Mukondiwa — **165**
Universal Usage — 166
Love is in it — 167
This too will come to pass — 168
Pregnant Rain — 170

Rosemary Chikafa-Chipiro — **171**
My Butterfly — 172
The Chandeliers in Your Eyes — 173
It Was Me — 174
You, Me and the Rain — 175
Rain Talk — 176

Rutendo Chichaya — **177**
Survival's Spine — 178
Dirty Linen — 180
Desires and Burdens — 182
Saturday 5 pm — 183
Home — 184

Ruvimbo Martha Jeche — **185**
Silent Prayers — 186
Tell Me the Old Story — 187
Roaring Woman! — 188
When Lola Left Home — 189
I Wanted to Write a Love Poem — 190

Samantha Rumbidzai Vazhure — **191**
there are no words — 192
Lullaby for a sleepy heart — 193
Bug of insurgence — 194
What sort of peace… — 195
Travelling by thought — 196
Blackbird's cry — 198

Shumirai Nhanhanga — **199**
Siblings — 200
Hello — 201
Talent — 202

Sibonginkosi Christabel Netha — **203**
A Meaningless Story — 204
There was a Void — 205
Bird of Paradise — 206

Twin Lollipops	208
Siphathisiwe Mitchel Lunga	**209**
Mother Nation	210
On Prayers	211
Scents and Stars	212
Foreign Accents	213
The Poem	214
Miracles	215
Sue Nyakubaya-Nhevera	**216**
Fragrances	217
Failing Feet	218
Time-travel	219
Childhood Feels Like Home	220
Wind	221
Tariro Ndoro	**222**
Hunting	223
Bodies	224
Thandokuhle Cleo Sibanda	**226**
Maybe, Maybe Not	227
A Lot Like Barbie	228
My Therapist Says	229
The Streets That Raise Us	230
It Won't Count	231
Tsitsi Ella Jaji	**232**
The Spread	233
moving mom to my brother's: an alzheimer's poem	234
Wadzanai Tadhuvana	**235**
Not Loved, Not Held	236
Dreams	237
The Burden of Culture	238
Zahirra Dayal	**239**
De-frizz, De-melanate, Diminish	240

Ubiquitous Fear 241
The Yellow House 242
Autumn 243
Where are you really from? 244
What do you mean racist? 245

Zaza Muchemwa **246**
She 247
Under Your Spell 248
'Not another political poem' 250
Psalms from Concrete 251
Manifesto 252
Rain Dance 254

Zenith Bvukutwa **255**
A Coffee and a Cigarette 256
Wish List 257
Again 258
Broken City 259
The Period 260

Disobedient Poetics—Translating the Third Space: An essay by Tariro Ndoro **262**

Bibliography **267**

Acknowledgements **269**

Afric McGlinchey

Afric spent her formative years in Ireland, Zambia and Zimbabwe. Educated at Rhodes University and UCT, she has lived for periods in Paris, London and Spain. Her début, *The lucky star of hidden things* was published by Salmon Poetry (2012). The recipient of a Hennessy Award, she was named one of Ireland's 'Rising Poets' in a special edition of Poetry Ireland Review. Afric's second collection, *Ghost of the Fisher Cat* (2016), was nominated for the Piggott, Poetry Now and Forward Prizes. Both collections were translated into Italian, published by Casa L'Arcolaio and showcased at the Italian Literature Institute in Dublin. A chapbook, *Invisible Insane* (SurVision) appeared in 2019 and *Hung Laundry and Certain Bodies* is forthcoming in 2023. In 2021 Broken Sleep Books published *Tied to the Wind,* a hybrid childhood memoir, for which she received an Arts Council of Ireland Literature Bursary. Afric lives in West Cork.

Birthstone

My father lays your jewellery on the table,
offers me first choice.
Its light seduces: from every angle

lightnings glide,
a compass with forty norths,
captured star.

I think of its birth, deep beneath
the Drakensberg,
then slipstreamed west

to the long Namibian shore;
deposited on pocket beach,
bedrock gully,

wind corridor; later,
hand-picked by smugglers.
An impulse to possess

this tear of the gods; now my legacy.
Neglected during conflict days,
almost, as with you, abandoned.

I recall those last weeks,
laughing at childhood memories,
taking your hand on a hospital bench,

twisting the ring on your too-thin finger.
I twist it now, on mine,
twirl my tongue over its cool surface,

until it sparks a different view –
and something in its light, a fleck,
reflects you back.

In my dreams I travel home to Africa...

...to the heat of early morning Harare,
hustle of the Sunday market, Shona handshakes,
loose and triple, palm to palm

where buses zig-zag pot-holes
big and black and bold enough to jump into;
white-robed worshippers gather under trees;

chongololo queues wait for pirate taxis;
men, dark as squid ink, drink chibuku,
women wrapped in java prints,

with swaddled babies, rock their backs,
sell plump bananas on laid-out sacks,
or sun-warmed avocados, each ample as a breast.

There's the pin-thin whine of mosquitoes,
then the silence – just before they bite;
drums beating bass into the pavement;

mbiras, jumpy, rhythmic;
voices calling *mangwanani, marara sei?*
cracks of thunder, clatter of blinding rain.

Willards chips, pungent, red-powdered;
tongue-curling kapenta; sadza nyama, hand-rolled;
Sparletta cream soda, green fizz in my nose;

melting tar and diesel fumes; dusty air,
burnt grasses of the vlei, heavy-scented petals
of yesterday,   today and tomorrow.

* *chongololo* – millipede
  chibuku – beer
  mbira – thumb piano
  mangwanani, marara se?i – Shona greeting (good morning, how did you sleep?)
  kapenta – a type of sardine
  sadza nyama – maize meal porridge with meat
  vlei – marshland

Last Conquest

You totter, shaking, to the bath,
bestow, like an ancient king,
a fluttering hand.
I lumber you up and in, no ceremony,
offer you a small gift of soap
and at your gestured dismissal,
withdraw to await
further instructions.

Summoned again, I avert
my eyes, and brace
so you can rise, lean on me;
at the rim, pause for breath,
cheeks glowing an unnatural red,
thinning hair flustered into wet shapes,
hazel eyes fixed
on some remote kingdom.

Then you heave,
a behemoth
surfacing from the undersea,
lift one limb, land, hold,
take an unquiet breath,
then swing the other,
bird-thin, bone-white,
over.

When you are restored
to a formal dignity,
we stand
side by side in the lift,
face tight-jawed doors,
and wait,
sorrow's invasion
borne in a tomb of silence.

White Sky

1
Outside, the sky is white as snow,
but there is no snow in Africa today,
not in Accra, Entebbe,
Addis Ababa or Zanzibar.
It's an impossibility, the idea
of blizzards, gales, aberrations
of winter, while we sit here,
hugging the heat to our pores.

The board flickers names:
Brazzaville, Lilongwe,
Kinshasa, Djibouti...
Our destination will land us
in the ice-chill, erase
all memory of this temperature,
the slow, languorous sway
of sun people.

2
Umbali wa mwisho wa safari—
Have a safe journey,
says my screen.
Newsflash
of an earthquake in Haiti—
all over our spinning planet,
weathers, shudders,
rocks, cracks.

3
We tip this way and that,
curving now
towards Youghal,
and already
Africa is melting away
as a caprice of light
flicks up totemic images,
Northern childhood memories.

On the soles of their feet

I revisit this Harare life that I have left:
new hair extensions, heels and shiny faces;
the guards with their batons guiding white
Mercedes between parallel lines;
potholes filled up hourly by street kids
who rob red bricks
from suburban garden walls;
dark windows that roll down, float
dollar notes for school fees.

The Book Café is closed, for fear
of revolutionary activity,
and Mannenburg's is shut down too:
all that jazz is quite suspicious.
The black streets rock
with drunken kombis; restaurants
have sprung up in the tranquil garden
of private homes, and look,
they're selling furniture, clothing, trinkets.

On New Year's Eve, the town feels empty;
friends have headed to Vic Falls,
taken off for Mozambique. But in this bar,
to an African beat, hips and buttocks sway boisterously.
A Roman candle spurts for half an hour,
like sporadic, bent-over laughter. Rain brings frogs
and lulls the crickets and scents swirl in and then
there's no electricity. You'd think there was a war,
or sudden peace, for all the expectation.

The drive across an unlit town,
son riding shotgun for protection.
A pre-dawn skinny dip among the frogs.
No lights; no water from the taps.
A solitary plane at the airport. But there are diamonds
and cutters and polishers and smugglers
and dealers right next to Eco-net and Buddy.
There are diamonds.
There are diamonds. And bodies.

Eighteen

When I was eighteen,
I swam four lengths under water;
he kissed me, told me he loved me.

I let him touch my breasts;
walked across the ridge of the sofa
as he proposed.

What would you have been,
my little one, who beat
inside me for five months,

remained nameless, have no grave.
Yet your presence is felt in wordless
whisper, and on this day, in sunshine,

rain, or fog, I listen for you, the hum
of your shape cradled between pelvic bones.
You would be eighteen.

Ashleigh Mafemba

Ashleigh (who writes under the pseudonym Leigh_Tigrexx) is a poet and psychology student. She started writing as a hobby at a very young age but quickly realised her passion for poetry specifically and focused on it. Her journey led her down a self-publishing path on Wattpad with her first three anthologies: *Whiffs Of Nostalgia, Claws & Cacti* and *MAGENTA*. Leigh is also the Founder and curator of a creative Trust called Bonzai Incorporeal which focuses on collaborative projects across diverse forms of creative expression including poetry, fashion and film. In light of her various creative passions, she has resorted to finding divergent methods of expressing her poetry, having ventured in spoken word and is currently working on visual and auditory variations to express her work

Two-faced

A coin has two faces

Heads and tails

I'm a coin made of different bases

Falling sometimes from different places

Non-fiction with a pinch of fairy-tale.

But when you look at me,

Do you see the traces

Of insecurities I've tried to hide?

Always seeking mercies

Waiting for a survival formula

to come with the tides.

I'm like a coin, but not of gold,

An alloy— two mixed components.

I'm hot and I'm cold

Vibrant and reactive like transition elements...

Being in my presence

Can be like walking on eggshells

Or floating on clouds

Like wailing sirens

Or chiming bells—

Two faces, a single coin.

Speaking in Tongues

And so you wonder what a person who hasn't died
Knows about dying.
I know a butterfly is a caterpillar
Before it starts flying,
Before life starts happening
Before the binds start tying.
The grave becomes my portal,
An architect immortal.
To build myself I had to be un-alive,
Until I purged myself
Of the need to survive.

My heart died to show me
That love is a calibre of delicacy.
My lungs gave in
So I could hold on for dear life...
But death doesn't scare me.
Death is just nature's second wife.
So I closed my eyes
Because my brain was going numb,
But like I said,
We ought to die, to become.
Where life breaks you down,
Death makes you humble—
I may be speaking in tongues
But I hope your false walls will crumble.

They don't write about us

They don't write about us;
We came face to face with angels,
Through mental death and social disease
Because we're surrounded by Cains dressed as Abels.
Befriending fear and jealousy
Because we've lost the keys
To peace
Now people of the law are lawless
Now humankind's souls are unstable
Lives where the directional arrows are aimless
Now our soils are red
Blood is the water we are being fed
And love is just another fable.

I said,
They don't write about us;
We came face to face with the truth,
Through visions of survival and pain
Re-defined,
We look weak and we've become hungry
For a different kind of youth.
What once was in black and white
When we were colour blind.
We've painted with pretty words,
While we sing our songs with a missing tooth
We'll paint our bodies
To show the colour of our minds,

Boys with hair like Samson,
Girls with the movement Ruth.

And the anthem is:
Just Be Kind.

Hymn of Rebirth

You don't need to utter words to talk
Or make a sound at all
You don't have to linger on the sidewalk
Or wait for me to call
Because silence has a funny way
of dancing with reality
And our insecurities they sway
On the waves of our minds
Creating voids within our mortality.

Often times we end our stories as strangers
How unkind
Yet with each fresh breath
Our lungs sing hymns of rebirth
Why not grow lilies between the spaces of our heartbeats
 —barren acres
While our wild hearts root themselves deep in the earth
Teaching our bodies to extend what we speak
We have modern tongues but still our souls are antique.
Learn – teach our minds not to dance to emotions
But be glided gracefully through the universe's ocean.
And perhaps a day will come when we speak as one again…
As the rainbow speaks to the rain.

Carla-Ann Makumbe

Carla-Ann is a writer who hails from Gweru, Zimbabwe. She is the author of the collection *And To Patricia I Had To Man Up* and recently released novel *Here's To Knots And Ties*. Some of her poems can also be found in the anthologies *Loud Thoughts* and Mukana Press's *Old Love Skin*. Carla-Ann derives her inspiration from society and is always willing to tackle issues most would whisper about. Equality and finding a voice for the modern girl child are among the issues that are close to her heart. Her writings echo inspiration and tackle social, economic, emotional and political challenges faced by the youth, and love. She is the editor of She Glows Africa Magazine.

My tales

Laughing exorcises these demons that constantly rise to my mouth as my ribs hold them down like a corset.

I envision the devil doing a little dance, a little tap there, a little tap here, wooing me to a vile dance that we have normalised call it a tango.

My stomach stirs as I hold a plate greasy full, my body screams I have reached its limits but healthy is expensive.

This is a game I lost long before I heard my mother's voice in her womb, long before I kicked her to let her know I live.

Mine is of goblins sprawled all over the floor as their hunchbacks become the constant hurdles I have to overcome.

Like an athlete I sprint but can only go so far as my body still screams limits!

Viruses are drawn to me like flies to a defecation that I have become as my eyes stare at the sky and I can see the big man smile on me.

Are mine curses or is it this strength that has opened demonic doorways as I am constantly stirred in a cauldron?

See mine is hard, the bed rock has nothing on it,

mine is a warrior's tale told to stir courage in offspring of royalty.

Mine is told by the scars on my body, it is the annunciation of a goddess reincarnated.

I will not let mine be washed by the Nile, if anything rivers would have to turn red before I drop my shield and armour.

I will celebrate every crack and crevice, every dance performed on hot ash as this Queen dances to her throne.

Mine are glorious!

Delirium

The sound of mills churning or is it a train approaching draws me in,

nowhere to land with time making its own tick tock noise.

My heart plunges into palpitations as I grope for solace. And just as my hand reaches out,

the strings of fate are rearranged, and I find myself back at the beginning of the maze.

The sounds of the mills churning or is it the train approaching or it's the sound of the clock at its steady pace tick tock.

The world opens to be my oyster and I am swimming.

Stroke after stroke as hope is revived within me.

Amidst it all I find love, I fall for love and just as I reach the peak, the string of fate strikes again,

to leave me yelping like a ballerina with a broken leg.

I have limped and stroked in this vast ocean yet here I am, spotlight on me but no cheers so the earth gives in to earthquakes and tremors,

finding myself amidst chaos with the sounds of the mill churning or is it the train approaching accompanied by the tick tock of the clock.

Chaos Reincarnated

Chaos, I can sense you in the breeze that jolts me back to reality on a hot summer's day. I can feel you in the soft whisper of mother earth as I surrender to cold shivers.

I can almost predict when you will swoop like an eagle and take what is yours from my life.

I can feel you announce your arrival in the rising pitch of my voice, hitting each note with operatic precision as the glass shatters into shards that pierce his face.

I know you have arrived as he starts to rage like Tshaka Zulu and even before he lashes out his stare is enough to provoke me, ancestors are summoned to this bull ring too.

My tongue begins to dance whilst the fire burns him slowly, a volcano waiting for the perfect moment to erupt.

I feel you envelop me, seize me, rip this gift from my arms and I embrace you with a deep exhale as you invade me.

I am left stripped and cowering in a foetal position as my throat tortures me with fires I have lit.

Until next time, Chaos, I whisper into the wind.

To the angel who watches over me

Some days the distance between us feels greater than an elephant, greater even than a stampeding herd.

Some days I feel the world crumbling all around me and there you are not leaving any space between us, not even the eye of a needle.

Some days I hear your voice in the wind and only after looking for you in faces that couldn't possibly be yours, does reality sink in.

Some days you are the sun that breaks after the storm and on other days I feel your absence.

Cyclones and hurricanes ravage through my life.

Some days you are a figment of my imagination as I don't remember your touch, but on other days you are present in everyone who ever met you.

The glimpse of your face in my memory fragments my heart into shards but your love restores me.

Some days you are the cheerleader whispering in my ear to go on and other days the deafening silence makes me aware of your presence. On those days
there is a dark hole within me, a vortex that sucks the life out of me.

On those days my voice just wants to be free and chant spells that would make witches cower.

On those days all things vile in me envelop me and I am but a dark cloud and then I think you once loved me.

On those days when anger subsides and loneliness dances around me, I acknowledge the orphan's song and affirm you are always with me.

Charity Hutete-Makawa

Charity is a Zimbabwean born author and performance poet. She is also a professional social work practitioner with an MSc and PGD in Social Work. Charity's body of work is an intricate mix of social commentary and undiluted intrapsychic dialogue. Her chapbook, *Undressing Under the Noon Sun*, was published in 2019 by Akashic Books as part of the New-Generation African Poets boxset series. Her works have been featured in several literary journals including New Contrast Review and The Kalahari Review; and showcased in numerous mixed arts exhibits at various international arts festivals, including but not limited to HIFA and Shoko Festival, Zimbabwe; Speak the Mind, South Africa; MIAF, Botswana.

How to birth an adult

I met Mai Mati mid-March 2018.
Before then, she didn't exist anywhere.
Not on any documentation,
not in a single memory.
She simply wasn't.

When she did arrive, everyone
addressed her with puzzling familiarity.
Each with opinions of how she ought to be,
ought to care for her unmentionables,
dress, eat, and behave now,
and more importantly, how
she was to mother.

I didn't like her much.
Each time she surfaced
I coiled further into myself.
She felt like a fraud.

Baba Mati showed up
about the same time.
Poor man, born with the weight
of a small family on his shoulders.

In a past life, he may have been
an MC or a poet afraid of the dark.
But this life demands he keeps a nine-to-five
and wakes to face burglars
when the alarm sounds.
When we met, we sighed hello.

Converted

Dad takes everything with
a pinch of salt. Just a pinch.
Mum devours.

When saved,
Daddy dabbled with benedictions
and two-line prayers before meals.

Mum shut down her shebeen,
traded her high afro and miniskirts
for yards and yards of white cloth
worn loosely over her frame,
complete with a headscarf.

The cloth spaced
words, distanced bodies
and estranged souls.

The one has become two.
Two silenced mouths
at opposite ends of the table,
two beds.

The Art of Smiling

I didn't have to teach it
what was expected of a woman
birthing in her late thirties.
It just knew.
Gratitude. FULL STOP.

And so, the scar
on my lower abdomen,
much like my face,
started smiling long before
its insides stopped bleeding.

And then it's not

The voice is crisp. And then it's not.
The frame is bold. And then it's not.
The skin is supple. And then it's not.
The womb tight. And then it's not.
The hair is dark. And then it's not.
The sleep is deep. And then it's not.
The vision is sharp. And then it's not.
The stride wide. And then it's not.
The smile is white. And then it's not.
The mind incisive. And then it's not.
First the focus is on all that's not.
And then it's not.

Love's Extras

She is everything
I expected and didn't.
She is buckets of mischief
and side steps too deep into my boundaries.
I'm tickled as I boot her out.

I'm what she expected and didn't.
I'm buttoned all the way to the top,
and won't breastfeed unless I'm alone.
I call her son by his first name,
and swat his bum whenever I like.

She is everything I expected and didn't.
She hails with bags of beans, maize meal,
and a live chicken with each visit.
She is a village in one, I'm from another.

Chioniso Tsikisayi

Chioniso is a writer, performer, poet and playwright from Bulawayo, Zimbabwe, whose primary mediums of expression are through spoken word, music, dance and storytelling. She was crowned the first runner up for the 65th Kenya Poetry Slam Africa Contest and placed third for the Intwasa Short Story Competition 2021. Her work has been featured in a selection of publications such as Brittle Paper, Isele Magazine, Litro Magazine, The Kalahari Review, Ipikai Poetry Journal, Agbowó art, AFREADA and *Intwasa Short Stories Volume Two*. In 2022, her debut play, *A Woman Has Two Mouths,* was shortlisted for the African Women Playwrights Network Festival of Plays held in Accra, Ghana. She won the Canopus Award 2023 for excellence in interstellar writing in the Original Local Short Form Fiction Category for her short story 'Gumbojena'.

Exchange Rate

Last night on the news another Zimbabwean man
was set alight.
Paraffin kiss,
body blackened from the hate,
flesh dripping candle wax for the nights Eskom left South African
homes in the pitch blackness of political tithes.
Bone, sinew, tissue.
The cracking of a whip against a salt and pepper sky.
Assault and pepper crimes.
Someone crying out for their mother in the midst
of an incinerator.
Xenophobic flames lighting up the disco ball of the sun
as bystanders look on
with eyes for surveillance cameras
and ears as satellite dishes broadcasting a murder signal
devoid of pity.

At the end of the month
there is no money to collect.
Not even a body or a bond note.
His mother stands at a Western Union branch
and receives the ashes of her son's remains.
The remittances of blood repatriated home.

Our forefathers never had funeral policies.
They bore children as insurance.
But what happens when a child dies before their parent?

A woman's womb smokes like a chimney at
the trauma of losing another child to the flames
of economic migration.
The biological tremors of a house built
on orphaned laughter.

where is our husband?
where is our father?
where is my son?

The Next Great Baker

Have you ever raised a child from a bowl of dried yeast?
This is how we grew up
    as self-raising orphans
sugarless
 when breadwinners died without warning.
    My mother's casket, a bread tin from whose oven womb
we sprang out like loaves of bread.
Hot, searing
   scones of grief,
freshly baked.
The crust of nearly blackened pastry.

Cremation.
   Creation.
 Milk, eggs, flour, sugar.
 My sister learned to bake a meaningful life with only half the ingredients of an
ailing economy.

Water and laughter,
Powered by the light of the sun.
The half-life of a radioactive mind.
Growing up a black girl is a kind of alchemy.
 Blackcurrant loaf
   banana bread of dreams deferred
raisin a daughter in the sun.

    Somehow she became a full woman
while I remained the waning moon of a girl
thin crescent lips half smiling to an eclipsed night
    sweet morsels of hope.
   Everyone is leaving the country
following the cookie trail of a better life
while we remember the dead.
  While we keep our grandmothers' home,
preservation of memory like crafting marmalade.
                       This is the legacy of bread
savouring the crumbs of a dying inheritance.

HardTalk

When I was ten I wanted to be an investigative
journalist.
Envisioned myself on BBC news a delicate figurine dressed in cargo pants
entrenched in the chaos of foreign lands.
"Hi, my name is Depression reporting live from a mid-twenties crisis."
I am twenty-four, a poet whose archives are full of bones.
My friends have university degrees while I bear the third-degree burns
of universal loss.
Aren't we all archaeologists of some distant painful past?
There is no end to this continuous digging.
Nineties baby, post-colonial living in the ruins
of a Great Zimbabwe.
Dambudzo's house of hunger,
haunted by the ghosts of graduates in search of employment
overseas.
This mouth is a graveyard and each time I speak your name,
I imagine flowers blooming on the tombstone that is my tongue.
Words are a resurrection of dead things.
My nation is a dead thing.
I am the undertaker of its corpse,
embalming the limbs that fell off the commonwealth leaving us in
common poverty.
Hold breath.
Hold Space.
    Hold breath in between the spaces and
in between the aching
chisel out of truth and tooth
a dentistry of Rhythm and Blues.
This is a case of Stares
leading to different points of view
spiralling upward into
the subconscious attic.
To glance fleetingly
into the master bedroom of bedlam.
Is there a soft place to lay our heads to
rest after the genocide?

Thunderstorms and Hibiscus Leaves

Sister,
you and I grew up too quickly.
The sun fell behind our backs and when it came round again we were twenty-one carrying a lifetime of tired.
Our milk teeth gone.
Pearls of pleasure embellished in the growing pains.
Make-up over the counter of a drug store, awakening to
teenage dreams.
Contoured face of pretty illusions.
Finding jeans to fit both body and soul of woman.
Mothering our baby brother from infancy to adolescence.
I told you I loved a boy and you laughed like a thunderstorm whose rain brings life.
This poem is a thunderstorm
an awkward stuttering record
laced with rhumba beats from a foreign summer.

Flash,
this poem is a snapshot of your beauty.
I am in awe of you.
I am in awe of us.
The flowers that grew from the concrete,
purple hibiscus leaves of melanin bodies stretching to the surface of
lightning.
Everything about us is striking.
    This is an awakening.

I Want to Fall Apart Quietly

I want to fall apart quietly
on a Sunday morning
in the corner of my blue bedroom,
with Pythagoras' theorem scrawled
across the walls in green marker,
the radio playing Sade,
the birds chirping their song,
the trees whispering secrets
between their sweet leaves
of the fruit ripening on my lips—
a kiss,
the sweetest taboo
of falling in love.

I want to fall apart quietly
inside Scripture and a cup
of coffee
dark enough to sip from the roots
of a rich ancestry,
sweet enough to not despise the origins
of pain or poverty
or generational trauma.

These are freshly ground aspirations,
the dreams percolating at the centre of
my mind.
The scent of ambition is heady.
It fills this room.
It climbs into my bed,
clings to my clothes
demanding to be felt.

So I fall apart in the hope that when I fall
back together,
my wholeness will proclaim itself loudly.

Planting is a Heavy Thing

Silver linings
streak the cloud of every broken
promise,
December rains
reminiscing the sweetness of summer.
The harvest of our hopes,
freshly cropped
from soil the colour of blood.

Planting is a heavy thing,
the roots of family trees sinking
deep into the underbelly of earth.
I think of my mother's stretch marks,
silver linings in a grey cloud,
soft like paintbrush strokes dipped
in the melanin of her skin.

Brown was the colour of the woman
who birthed me,
brown was the colour of the body
that housed me,
brown was the colour of my grandmother's hands
as she ploughed and watered her farmlands.

I am learning to unlearn the language of regret.
I am learning to unlearn a lifetime of pain.
Planting is a heavy thing,
but I am the seed of woman.
I am the unbroken promise of love.

Cristol Danai Mubaiwa

Cristol is a poet based in Harare, Zimbabwe. Born in Mutare and raised in Harare, she has felt inspired and challenged by the two cities' energy. Cristol`s love for poetry began in High School after taking on rap that eventually morphed into poetry, both page poetry and spoken word poetry. Cristol draws inspiration from raw emotions of her personal experiences and social issues. Cristol explores identity, gender, culture, human connection amongst others. She regularly performs at open mic and also curates events for other artists to have a platform to showcase their talents. She has performed locally at HIFA, Shoko festival, amongst others, and international performances with Paza Sauti`s Poems of the start of the world and The accelerator for Gbv prevention. Cristol's dream is to one day see her words in print, inspiring readers with her unique perspective and love for language.

No Byes My Love

Yes the world is loud and this life is drowning I just want to drown next to you

Heavy is the heart that beats away from its half
Soft are the lips that are kissed often
Coffins are places some hearts heal
The heart feels
Feels what the body fails to put into song
No melody when lyrics become lost in seas of emotion
Waves
They come and go
They call it pain
Shows you're sane
Raves my mane
So again
Let's pretend
That the seas turn pacific
Allow us to breeze like cigarettes
Like a high that scratches the itch
No byes my love
No byes

Period

Imagine being a woman
Having a rainforest of a body with roots that shift to your stomach
They dance to the moon at least five sunrises each month
They call it period
As in full stop
Yes period
As in end of the sentence
So tell me how many of those should women go through before the patriarchy understands that saying no is a complete sentence that needs no explanation
Period.

It's amazing how we barely breathe when we laugh, or cry, or cum!
Coming to a conclusion of a body that can bleed
For birth
For death
For growth
Vagina!
The first and last to spit you out
Let it bleed
That body deserves leave days for all that work please!

Behind The Curtains

Oh if you could see behind these curtains
You would see how happy we are
You'd see the sad parts too that are usually followed by forehead kisses and makeovers
You'd see our teeth
How they wave in greetings each time our lips spread
But mostly because of her
Mostly because her joy fills up my spaces with music and motion
Like the happy drug

But see where I come from hetero minds are holy
They go to temples and get sealed for exaltation
Where I come from
Mothers hang medals on their necks for each daughter that gets married
Give themselves a pat on the back
Like they did a good job raising a daughter that someone's son
Would choose for a wife
And life
Is about society's spectrum of thoughts
Like colours make the world too bright
Like black doesn't exist on the rainbow so the rainbow can't exist in me

These thorns are starting to make my feet bleed
My strides are getting shorter and I want to leave

Oh if you could see behind these curtains
You'd know
How emotion commands purity
And I want to give her pure love
I want to love her when she's depressed
Ecstatic, goofy, disgusting, smiling
I wish I could do that with no judgment
Even from her

Ooh you should see her behind her curtains
That I am not allowed to open sometimes
Most times
Cognitive dissonance I hear
The teachings whisper in her ear
I have learnt to love her in her cage
Just like how hearts beat close to the ribs
I can barely breathe
I wish I could set her free but she's packed away the key

We were taught things
That unlearning is disbelief
That this kind of love isn't natural
So I hold myself with ropes,
Fastening parts of myself down because they mustn't be seen
Sometimes I fail
Trying to breathe under the sea of my emotions
And this might just be my most honest poem
A cry of devotions
Tears are prayers when the soul is too tired to speak

Oh you should see me behind my curtains,
Thoughts throbbing to burst into fruit
This garden of my being needs water
Needs sun
Needs air
Needs earth
You should see how I become planet
How I become the definition of space
You would see these tears
Coursing down my cheeks

Hoping for the day I won't have to hide behind these curtains

Mhamha

Our mothers are poems
Poems unwritten
The context is simple
Our mothers are us with experience

I've seen seeds in my mother's palm
Seeds that sprouted and grew enough to be served on a platter
I've seen bare dust become beautiful gardens by the hand of my mother
How dare you not see the magic
The magic on our mothers' tongues to spit seeds into our ears but they live in the gardens of our subconscious
The seeds that grow to thought because what they speak we believe
Well sometimes
Because mom so much has changed since
But I don't blame you
I don't blame you because your experiences carved your thought process and removed certain pages in the book
They removed the pages to keep you here mhamha
To keep us here mhamha

I've seen you being silenced with a gaze
Society sealed your lips and encouraged you to swerve only your hips
They say women lie but them hips don't lie
Put a value on you as a housewife
Patriarchy's beautiful queen
You say I sound angry

I had so many questions mhamha
I needed answers
Sometimes I think I sound angry because when a woman speaks it's considered her last stroke
She should have been burning to express her thoughts because otherwise why would she
And I have a lot to say mhamha
Like how your life could have been better
But sometimes bad things happen to good people

And it's always been us
So maybe that's why I'm angry mhamha
Because they taught you to be quiet
Say it shows humility, resilience and respect
I feel it here
And so it comes out here
But bhoo here moms? Kusekerera zvinhu zvisku fire

I get pregnant with these metaphors for all the poems our mothers could have written
These words are testimonies to all the parts of themselves they sacrificed to be perfect
To be worthy
To be respectable
To dismiss themselves
Sometimes
Sometimes they roar until the jungle earthquakes into pieces,
And in those moments seas of joy drown my sadness because wow
How majestic
You are majestic mhamha

* "bhoo here moms? Kusekerera zvinhu zvisku fire" is Shona slang for "everything ok, mom? Smiling at things you're not happy about".

Cynthia Rumbidzai Marangwanda

Cynthia is a Zimbabwean poet and award-winning author. She is the granddaughter of Shona novelist J.W. Marangwanda, one of the earliest published African writers during Zimbabwe's colonial period. Cynthia is a well-known spoken word poet and slam poet, performing under the moniker FlowChyld since 2008. She has performed at Poetry Africa (Harare edition), Poetry International Festival in The Netherlands, Harare International Festival of the Arts, Shoko Festival, LitFest Harare, Page Poetry Alive, among others. Her poems have been published by Brittle Paper, Badilisha Poetry X-Change, as well as in anthologies by Zimbabwe Cultural Centre of Detroit, Povo Afrika, and more. She is the recipient of a Zimbabwe National Arts Merit award for Outstanding First Creative Published Work for her debut novella *Shards* in 2015.

Birth

I give birth to myself
every time I refuse
to let them annihilate my spirit
or confine my worth
to the land of the lifeless.
I birth myself through agony and tears
the same way I birth lineages.
I am new life
Reborn in every struggle.

Echoes

I hear echoes calling
Instructing me to awaken the souls of ancestors
And bring them back to life
To walk on city pavements
To energise concrete avenues.

I feel like a conduit of those that have gone before
They find expression in the rhythms of ngoma, mbira and kora
In this age we their children
Inherit centuries and legacies of rebellion, riots and rage
We were chosen to be convention-breakers
To be creators and imagination-wakers
The Babylon system can never take us
Can never erase us
The beautiful African ones finally born
Reincarnations of our grandmothers and forefathers
Our heritage and history are the ammunition we use
To defend and contend for the sake of future seeds.

* Ngoma, mbira and kora are African musical instruments.

Stone Mansion

A mansion of stone
cemented by family bonds
too damaged to stand
The foundation is shifting
Built in 1980
Crumbling in the 21st century
The golden chandeliers illuminate
the cracks in the ceiling.

At least some remnants
of the original design still stand
At least it has not collapsed completely
Its granite rooms still echo
with some semblance of activity
The servants still glide through its corridors
obediently, desperately
The owners' flinty eyes
still watch over everything
Suspiciously.

Such is daily life
In these ruins masquerading
As a great house of stone.

Remembrance

Our bodies are vessels of eternity—
We are not just flesh
We are timelessness in motion
God has a home in the confines
of our physical beings
Yet we have forgotten
the infinity of our nature
because of too much time spent
in the density of matter.

The universe finds expression through us—
We are divine poetry written
in the language of the stars
Our origins are calling us to remember
that we are descendants of the heavens
Our essence is much higher than this Earth
We are the Creator's most profound work.

Our spirits transcend the limitations of humanity
This world is too small to contain us
We are cosmic beings inhabiting the world
in Bantu form
How can we die when our souls remain ageless?
We are ancient potential manifested in the present
We exist above time
but allow minutes and seconds to keep us in bondage
We search for the divine
even as it watches us every day from the mirror.

We must forget our amnesia
and start the process of remembering
We are eternity painted in black skin.

Our bodies are channels of divinity
We are more than flesh
We are timelessness in motion
God finds existence in the borders
of our physical lives
The time for remembering is now
The time for remembering is now.

Sista Outsiders

I would often see her
in the usual places, the mutual spaces
where subcultures converged
our worlds never quite merged
although our universes ran parallel
she was on that Afrocentric, pro-Ethiopian tip
I was more on that wanna-be hippie
trying to be bohemian tip
so we were kind of opposites
who both used our microphones as conduits
for a higher muse
it often felt like I was a student
and she was the master
the times I watched her on stages
she was the queen, so regal and radiant
I knew I could never surpass her
so I mentally saluted every time I passed her
she never really knew
how much I respected her craft
or the fire in her heart
I paid my tribute in secret and that was cool
until the day I heard the news
that this lioness had gone back to her Maker
she had surrendered her toil
and returned to the soil
leaving behind parts of her
that were too vital to die
creations of brilliance sculpted by the mind
of a genius-goddess
but almost immediately
rumours began to swirl
about her mysterious ways in the world
some said she lived unholy and unwise
others said she was a woman wild
that she belonged to the tragic tribe

that's why the devil got to her mind
and possessed her to take her own life
I heard all the talk
but couldn't bring myself to judge her demise
because I never walked a metre in her sandals
and I had no idea about her hustle
or her struggles
but I know a thing or two about pain
and I wish she would have called me
or told me
we could have talked about our demons
our inner aches
about the parts of existence that really, really hurt
about feeling young, gifted and cursed
about the beautiful seeds we had carried and birthed
who we feared we had tarnished with our ugly
maybe if we had talked
opened up, unravelled ourselves
sista to sista, outsider to outsider
she might have chosen not to set herself free
for infinity.

Loud

It is said a woman
who uses her voice too much
is not desirable, or decent.
I must be the most undesired
woman in the world then,
and the most indecent.

Deborah Nyasha Kabongo

Deborah is a half Congolese, half Zimbabwean artist. She is a self-published author with two books, *Scented Coffins* and *IamObliage*. As a self-taught writer she takes a narrative approach, with fusions of lyrical poetry. She has been writing since the age of ten and it has been a therapeutic way for her to express in metaphors her feelings and childhood experiences.

She is also a dancer by profession, and this has contributed greatly to the way she writes in expressing the body motion of her characters; she says, "dance is poetry in the flesh". She recently obtained her Honours degree in Sports Science and Management, focusing on Kinesiology.

The Dancer and the Filmmaker (Cumcorder)

I want you to make love to me through the lens
Spilled shades of red passion in the heat of the lights, camera, come and act on it
Caress my humps and bumps, black and white in 60s movies
Dip in and out, short films and screenplays, make I write a play
Script INT. Nips screaming out, they float like polaroid
My point of view, your viewpoint, both imbued with a dark sense of serenity
Soaking all these negatives, I'm wet, yes I'm all moist, I mean I'm almost there, don't stop
Give me that steady love gimbal, not like clanging cymbals
Smell my palm, without a scented coffin
Make me curl my toes and moan
With only just a cumcorder

Secrets the Garbage Man Knew (Madhodhabhini)

You would think they were walking out of a Lamborghini at Formula One—
Hands off the truck handle, they leap into a perfect landing "jog-strut-walk-slow down".
This ancient truck was tracing the tracks I left by my flower bed every morning.
Strands of last night's linguine peek from the lid of my rusty trash can.
The "clean-up crew" or "garbage men" or "trash collectors"
Madhodhabhini horait, I'm thinking Dirty Martini, he caught my eye, he wasn't dirty but he wasn't clean either.

You would think he had been air dropped from Italy, Cape Town or a metaverse that invented fashion before he was born.
That work suit sat on him like a fashion week dungaree, draped across one shoulder.
He grabs the "saga", this was still the ghetto and we recycled the life out of those saga bags,
He grabs the "saga", empties it and brings it right back where he picked it up.
There was a rhythm to it, as if he was sending me a message, call him the garbage postman, still Madhodhabhini.

You would think I was about to leave with the garbage truck and today was the day.
Every day I'd wake up early, wash up curly, just to watch this man take away my trash, make I ask for a ride, nearly—
"You could say hi, you know. The dirt will wash off just like that beauty mask you keep on overnight."
That hit hard, I sniff my own breath, he may have been right, he just reached a new level on my sexy scale.
Then a loud "wakanganwa lunchbox yako iwe" and "ko mari yemuriwo, tokuzivai munononoka kudzoka pakati peweek kudai" followed by a hush.
Reality snaps, the truck vapes, a stench fills the whispering air with secrets the garbage man knew.

* "Madhodhabhini horait" – "garbage man, ok then".
  "saga" – bin bag.
  "wakangwanwa lunch box..." – "hey, you've forgotten your lunch box/ packed lunch".
 "Ko mari yemuriwo, tokuzivai munononoka kudzoka pakati peweek kudai" – "what about money for vegetables? We know your tendency to come back late, especially midweek.

Photograph

I'm not just another brick in the wall
This nail you hammered in me
Loosens each time your fist hits the wall
I carried this image on my parole

I snapped a series of photographs with my eyes
You signed a series of autographs, a couple of hi's
The photo editor distorted your look
And now I don't know how you even look

Past the signs, the negative lines
If you look inside, you know you're mine
I saved the negative ones, with wine
I sit and drink to count there's nine

We still have eight tries
At night the cat cries
I raise this tripod to the tip of my toes
To snap another image before he goes

Ethel Irene Kabwato

Born in Mutare, Zimbabwe, Ethel trained as a high school teacher and holds a BA in Media Studies. She was selected to participate in the British Council Crossing Borders Writers Project in 2004. Kabwato has been featured in important anthologies that have shaped literary spaces in Africa and the world, such as *New Daughters of Africa* (Margaret Busby, Myriad Press), *Sunflowers in Your Eyes* (Menna Elfyn, Cinnamon Press), *Poetry International Website* (Rotterdam, Netherlands), *Writing Free* (Irene Staunton, Weaver Press), and *Ghetto Diary* (Zimbabwe Publishing House), an anthology that was selected as a set book for advanced-level literature students in Zimbabwe. Her poetry is included in *Between Two Rocks*, (Ben Gaydos, Flint University) in collaboration with the Zimbabwe Cultural Centre in Detroit (ZCCD). She has read her work at several institutions including Highway Africa Media Conference, Rhodes University and the University of Witwatersrand, South Africa. She has also been a guest of Cinema without Borders at the Movies That Matter (Human Rights) Film Festival in Amsterdam. She has participated in a reading and discussion of her work at the Hay Festival in Wales, UK and at Litfest in Harare. Kabwato is passionate about working with children and youths from disadvantaged communities and works with Slum Cinema, a voluntary initiative to empower youths through multi-media work.

In Remembrance

For Steve Sinosi Kabwato (1928 – 2021)

Dear Baba,
In remembrance of a great tree
That remains anchored in our hearts
In remembrance of greatness and strength
In memory of a tree whose giant trunk
Sturdy and resolute
Could weather any storm
In memory of a tree whose leaves
Withstood the harshest winters
And never fell from grace
In remembrance of a tree whose branches
Spread across nations but never wilted in the hottest summers
In memory of a great tree
Whose roots are deeper than any ocean
And not shaken by the winds of change
Nor uprooted by giant waves
This giant tree has birthed seeds of greatness
The seeds are in the heart and soul
Of the young people you see today
Lighting candles
In remembrance of sheltered dreams
Endless love
Unlimited possibilities
And a rich legacy of storytelling
In remembrance of a giant tree
That no axe can ever cut
No wind can ever sweep away
A tree that continues to grow in our hearts
And live on in our memories
In remembrance of a man who loved life
And life loved him back…

* Baba means 'father' in Shona.

Mothers and Babies

For Kirstin Pagels-Mbohwa and Claudia Mahachi

With babies slung on their backs
the way our mothers
used to carry their own babies
they stood under the *musasa* trees
rocking their children to sleep.
The African winter sun
smiles on them,
its serene beauty casting light
on the shadows of their dreams,
defining their existence
in the midst of scarcity.
Far away from the bright city lights
the sunflower by Claudia's doorstep
waves to the fading winter sun…
dances with the wind
and colours the lullabies
the mothers have carried
across oceans.
The wind gathers the words
they sing under the *musasa* tree:

> 'Hush-a-bye, baby, on the tree top,
> When the wind blows the cradle will rock;'

in this place they now call home….

Mother of the Revolution

You were not a winter woman.
When we met in April
on Independence Day
you said were a summer woman.
Removing winter's ice-cold shackles
and shaking the icicles
from your frost-bitten feet,
you said you held in your hands
the strength to bring
the sun into our lives.

You said you had lifted
your weary feet
from the ground.
You said you would meet me
at Freedom Square...
our only symbol of hope;
as we lift our voices high
in song and make our anthem rise
above the cold grey buildings
where the chairman and his deputies
sit in hunched silence
gulping cups of black coffee
as they seal our fate.

They said we were not heroes.
The party agreed that we were not villains
or sell outs, either...
They said we were just misguided women
who had thrown away skirts and aprons
in the Mukuvisi River
to join the long march...

Over steaming cups of black coffee
they wrote down the names of the martyrs

...the sacrificial lambs...
The wind carried your voice
above the acacias, jacarandas
and flamboyant trees
and shook their black hearts...

For sixteen days now
I have gone back to Freedom Square.
I have searched for your footprints
in the red soils where we once stood.
I walk slowly, bearing photographs,
savouring every step,
every memory of that summer.
I tell the image I hold
of what was once you;
that a sniper's bullet
at Freedom Square broke the march.
That is when I saw you
turning to face them
while we turned our backs on you...

This April I will go on a pilgrimage
to Freedom Square
with your photograph.
Maybe you may turn up.
Maybe someone who knows
what happened to you
might come, too...
Maybe the revolution itself might confess
that it 'ate you up'...
while the 'architects' of our freedom
raised their coffee mugs
and red velvet cake
in celebration of your demise
as they closed
another chapter of our history.

For Creedence
(1973 – 2013)

I thought I would write on your Facebook wall
as I used to every year,
and tell you that 38T is still home;
that Antonio, the mechanic
still wears his size 10 slippers
from Bata Shoe Company;
that they no longer watch
Buddy Spencer and Terence Hill
at Dangamvura Beit Hall.
Archford, the school bully,
is now a cobbler,
ZUPCO buses no longer
use the Dangamvura route
so 'Razorman' is no longer
a bus conductor.
Shaky 'Masamoosa' is no more;
his children do not make
samoosas as they used to
during his time
but his son, 'Jake Roberts'
is now a politician.
Unlike his father
he is in the opposition.
After Barbara 'Mafete' (she of the
vetkoeks by the school gate),
no one has ever taken her place...
no one sells vetkoeks anymore.
Rujeko School, our alma mater,
still stands
but the uniforms have changed...
I thought I would let you know
that Barbara is back in Germany now
...and I still remember the day she danced
and sang along to yesteryear

hits from Creedence Water Revival
at the Jameson Hotel.
We would have given anything
to see you again...
argued, fought (with words)...laughed...
visited places... ate... drank... argued... watched a good film... talked.

Whispers in the Dark

I am afraid of the whispers
In the dark
I am afraid of the silence
That greets me on the township streets
I am afraid of people
Who knock on our door at night...
During the day
I am afraid of the people
I talk to every day...

The young police officer who gives us a lift
Every morning...
He likes discussing politics
And makes sure to study
The consternation on our faces
In the rear-view mirror
As we fumble for bond coins
In our bags to pay him later
On arrival in the city...

Masimba, the army recruit
Whose appetite for cough medicine
Is unmatched...

Baba aSuzeni the township reveller
Who is also the party's Ward 13 councillor...
...everyone knows where to find him
From 9 to 5pm...
Mukoma Keni, the barber
Who plies his trade under the musau tree
Whose bark carries an iron plate placard
With a huge, rusty nail...
Roughly painted, *'Tinogera'* in red...
As he carefully cuts his clients' hair
He tells you all the 'latest' news

He has heard... he even repeats
What you have also told him in the past...

Chihera...
(Everyone calls her by her totem)
She is the township vendor
Who wears party regalia even at the market
When she is doing her business
Just in case duty calls
And she has to attend the burial of a hero...
...a cell meeting
Or if the chairman calls for
The distribution of seed and fertilizer
She never fails to tell every child who passes by:
'Tell your mother we have pumpkin leaves today!'

Sisi Giro...Gloria, to her clients...
Our big township sister of the night
And a hairdresser cum beautician
During the day...
She seems to take an interest
in Mukoma Keni's clients
Who sit under the Musau Tree barber shop
Waiting for their turn to get a haircut...
She continuously fidgets with her blonde wig
Her fake red nails dangerously poised
Mid-air in feigned innocence...
Her legs show that
Once upon a time she was just like us,
 Dark skinned...
...her bleached skin matches the colour of her wig...
She can be heard at every two-minute interval
Shouting out loud at women passing by
'Huyai tiruke musoro uyo, askana...manails tinoita futi!'
She chides them for staying too long
With the same hairstyle...

...Sister Maria,
The born-again church usher
Who sometimes graces the church pews
With her police uniform and baton stick
When she sings and dances
While collecting tithes and offerings
Our hearts, tortured with amnesia...
Melt with forgiveness
For the violence she and her colleagues unleash
...before and just after elections...
We tell ourselves that
'We have all sinned...'

Then there's Mukoma Jairos,
Popularly known as 'The Jackal'
By the old timers in the township
He is the businessman who owns
A supermarket, a bottle store and a butchery
At the shopping centre named after
His father who was also known as Jai,
We just call the whole shopping centre,
Including the shops that are not his, 'KwaJai...'
It is said he inherited the business
From his father who collapsed
And died
On the day he lost his Ward 13 seat to BaSuzeni...
It is said his father's ghost
Is often seen wandering around the premises
Past midnight...

The most interesting township dweller
Is the township school headmistress' boyfriend...
No one knows him by name
Younger than the head teacher,
Everyone calls him 'Ben 10'

No one talks to him about anything
Except pool...
His business is to play pool...

He seems to enjoy the mysterious aura around him:
'...Doesn't frequent Mukoma Keni's barber shop...
...doesn't entertain BaSuzeni, the councillor...or Sisi Giro...
...no fixed abode...he picks up and drops the head teacher on her doorstep...
...no gainful employment...smartly dressed...drinks moderately...
...doesn't smoke...wins every game of pool...doesn't have friends...when he talks,
...it is with such finality that it stuns the hearer into silence...'

Deep in our hearts, we know
And we are convinced that we know
Who he is but we don't talk about it...

Every secret in the township
Remains in the treasure chest
Of the heart...
When we do whisper,
It is to offer a prayer to the Most High
That the hedge we have put around
Our township house
Is fortified by His presence
During the day and at night...

---

* *'Tinogera'* means 'We cut/barber hair' in Shona.
  'Huyai tiruke musoro uyo, askana...manails tinoita futi!' – 'Come, let us braid that hair girls...we do nails also!'

Africa Day

We seem to be living our African dream
On the edge...
We celebrate our African-ness
On the streets that they have named
After the fathers who fought colonialism
These are the roads
That we also have trudged on
And their pot-holes mirror
Our fragile democracies...
And the depth of the promises
They made at independence...
The sign-posts are fading, too...
Just like the history they have sought to create...
Kwame Nkurumah...Samora Machel...Julius Nyerere...
Nelson Mandela...
Kenneth Kaunda...Sam Nujoma...
Are remembered in Harare
Through the streets that shelter us
When the presidential motorcade's bikers
Race past Samora Machel Avenue
Down Julius Nyerere
And past the bronze statue
Of Mbuya Nehanda, the nation's spirit medium...
...in the melee, just near the fly-over
On Kenneth Kaunda Avenue/Julius Nyerere Street
We try to count
The hundreds of bond notes
Needed to pay school fees
For the young dreamers
Who still carry the hope of the continent's dream...

We struggle with our conscience
When we try to remember
The women whose place in history
Has been forgotten...

Today, the women's fate
Lies in the hands of those
Who steal the African child's dream
On Africa Day and any other day
Of the year he attempts to leave
The home that has made him a stranger
...an unemployed tool
Fit only to become a couch potato
Whose skilled hands
Have mastered the art of holding
The TV remote control
...and whose mouth takes in anything
Thrown his way...
The mothers cradle their sons' and daughters'
Fractured dreams in their hands...

* Africa Day is celebrated every year on the 25th of May.

Fikile Sithembiso Mkandla

Fikile is a student doing her studies in Biochemistry and Biotechnology. Poetry is one of her passions. She has recently started working on spoken word poetry and has also had some of her pieces published. In late 2022, her poem "A piece of peace, please?" was published in the GCED *Poetry 4 Peace* anthology. This stands as her second published work, her first being a short story that was included in the *Lockdown Blues and Blisses* short story collection which was published in 2021. Fikile desires to speak through her literary work, especially on issues concerning mental and emotional health, to raise awareness of these areas.

Kuvelaphi?

The whirlwind churned in my mind overnight
bursting through my walls, lifting all my furniture
turning my fourteen-year-old house into a ramshackle wreck
a fixer-upper, unfamiliar even to the owner

*Kuvelaphi? – *Where is this coming from?* (isiNdebele)

Kum'nyama lapha!

Darkness, it's so easy to slip into again, isn't it?

To be called back by miscellaneous whispers into your "comfortable space".

Little do we realize that this is the old toxic friend, the one who left you with more scars than there are grains of sand.

*Kum'nyama lapha! – *It is dark here!* (isiNdebele)

Escape

I never thought hope had such a rowdy enemy.

I never thought letting the light in would make the darkness more menacing.

I never thought that it took just one step into true warmth, true love, true honesty.

Positivity.

Prayer.

Undaunted, I trudge on for I know there is truly something better.

And oh, the peace, wonderful peace,

Where have you been?

Fungai Rufaro Machirori

Fungai is a world traveller, essayist, poet and thinker. She is a co-author of *Sunflowers In Your Eyes: Four Zimbabwean Poets* and her non-fiction writing has appeared in the Guardian, the Mail and Guardian, Africa is a Country, and other platforms. Fungai is also a digital and social media creator, having founded Her Zimbabwe – Zimbabwe's first women's web-based platform – in 2012. She currently explores African digital cosmopolitanism, an original conceptualisation of hers in which she situates African digitality as global. She runs a podcast which further explores social and cultural aspects of technology. Fungai enjoys experiencing wonderment in the everyday and writes, creates and posits from this standpoint

Re-entry

I feel myself
Re-enter me
The sensation of me
A soft coat
Forgotten
For too many winters
Still the same
Shape
Same style
Same form
Giving in all the right places
Loose but close
Warm and cool
A pattern woven
From my very own yarn

The Imposition

A clutch of Watchtowers in hand,
she begins her attempt to convince me
that if I do not let her in
to save me,
I will condemn myself
to eternal suffering.

I tower over her as
I squint into her determined eyes,
spears of morning sunshine the backdrop
of our holy war.

She has rung the intercom thrice,
its noise an insistent siren;
a call to arms
until at last, I have stood before her at my gate
guarding the battleline between us.

She brushes the brim of her sunhat
unfazed by the heat,
riddling out her inquisitions:

DON'T YOU QUESTION THE UNFAIRNESS IN THE WORLD?

ARE YOU NOT AFRAID OF WHAT COMES AFTER THIS LIFETIME?

My nonchalance is polite,
but she pays this armour no heed,
determined to find a fault line
until
at last,
I declare to her that I do not see the world

as she does,
and do not want to.

She yields

slowly,
finally
begins to retreat from the border
she has failed to invade,
booklets still held up to her chest
like an armour plate

she thinks she has won
something:
a medal of honour or distinction perhaps.

She has not.

Because I know I have battled enough darkness,
fought enough foes
to feel fear at any more of them to come
in every lifetime and realm and world
that may follow.

Night Harvesters

Like witches,
We await the night;
Our ritual to harvest
Water and power
Trickling
Into near-barren pipes and sockets
In the midnight hour.

To sleep is to miss this short season
Of riches;
Is to live out a
Day of lack and remorse,
No gadgets powered up,
No buckets refilled.

So instead, we Sorcerers
Waken to howl at midnight's mirth,
Making merry of the menial
Casting spells of survival over our homes
Transmuting strife into sustenance.

undone

the past keeps
biting at the hem
of my dress
undoing
enough stitches
fraying
enough fabric
reminding me
how undone
i can become

KFC on a Friday Night

He comes up to my window,
The neon light of a 21-piece-bucket meal
Lighting his features like a cruel halo;
His washed-out red cap
Worn at an angle,
A black jacket draped loosely
Across hopeless shoulders.

Bleary drunken eyes
Watch me over the sound of my burring engine.

He asks for
A dollar;
Some help to get something to eat.

My response is shamelessly rehearsed,
Perfected by my many years of similar engagements.

Sorry sha, handina mari.

I look in my rear-view mirror,
Half-expecting his darkening form to return
As he moves on to the next driver behind me.

I listen again to his plea
As the attendant recites my order:

*So that's a Streetwise Two, four Zinger wings and a Coke,
Anything else M'am?*

The dollar eludes him again.

Yes, actually. Please change the Coke to an Oreo Krusher.

---

*Sorry sha, handina mari. – Sorry, mate, I don't have any money.

Seven

I wonder what your names are,
What your parents called you
Before or after they met you;
Before, as their hopes for you burgeoned
As your limbs formed flesh about them;

After they met you,
As your fists failed to unfurl.

I hope they got to dress you
In those clothes that were supposed to cleave
To your tiny forms
As you made your journey into life.

I hope they dressed you warmly
To counter your cooling blood
To adorn your entry into the next realm
As you left this world you never knew.

Seven, they say, is a perfect number.
Seven perfect souls.

I hope they named you
To forgive our forgetting
That you too were here
Briefly,
Cruelly.

Note: Seven babies were stillborn at Harare Central Hospital in one night in 2020 during the COVID pandemic as a result of delayed treatment, because of staffing issues relating to a lack of protective equipment and other mismanagement.

Gertrude Mutsamwira

Born and raised in the captivating landscapes of Manicaland, Zimbabwe, Gertrude, a 63-year-old "poet in progress", has always been deeply connected to the rich traditions and natural beauty that surrounded her. Growing up in a close-knit community, Gertrude was instilled with a profound appreciation for the power of storytelling with her first introduction to poetry being in 1978 when she translated a poem into English for a school magazine.

However, it wasn't until later in life that she discovered her true passion for poetry and the written arts. Following a diverse career path that included working as a teacher, counsellor and founding her own counselling service practice, she found solace and inspiration in the written word during the COVID 19 shutdowns worldwide. Drawing from her experiences and the vivid memories of her upbringing, Gertrude's poetry became a vessel for her to express the nuances of the life of a married Zimbabwean woman, the struggles people faced during the COVID 19 shutdowns, and the profound connection between humans and their resilience to persevere despite the odds they face.

Now, with her evocative verses capturing the hearts of readers, Gertrude stands as a testament to the enduring power of artistic expression for her generation, proving that one's true calling can be discovered at any stage in life. A dream come true for her.

Lost Love

You have lost it haven't you?
You took her for granted and assumed she would never do anything by herself.
To you she was a ragdoll, an object you would treat with contempt.
You could break her soul, kill her spirit, destroy her self-esteem and paralyse her self-confidence.
Yet you could tell the world how much she meant to you, but you never told her directly.

To the world you would boast of your children's achievement,
Forgetting the role she has played in raising them.
Why dress her down in front of them?
Why spite her and show them how lowly you perceive her?
As if not enough, at family gatherings you showed your controlling freakiness by denigrating her.
Each time she tried to air her voice, you would block her by punching her to quietness. At times dragging and forcing her to the bathroom, dipping her face into hot water. Why do it?
Many times she would pass out and be resuscitated by you drenching her with cold water.
You commanded her how to reply when the kids asked about the blue eyes and welts on her back.
Each time you gave her grocery money,
You requested she bring the receipts and change, lest she pinched it.
Every cent you gave her, evidence had to be shown and she obliged.
She had so much love for you.
Many times, friends would tell her to leave but she wouldn't because you are the father of her children.
Despite all the treatment, she would still cook, iron and provide for you.
Was that not good enough?

She would also cover up for the bruises you inflicted on her.
"Oh, I bumped and fell against something," she would say.
Deep, deep inside she was hurting and you chose not to see.
Of late she ceased to complain and you thought you had her where you wanted her.
I cannot believe you are crying over her now because she has left you.
You can't accept she has found someone who loves her for who she is.

Joblessness

You had it, now it's gone!
That which you cherished and loved so dearly is gone.
Gone it has, you don't have it now.
It is hard to comprehend, hard to come to terms with and fathom it.
It is hard to accept, the thought of it bounces on the head refusing to sink in.
"Help me before I lose my marbles, for I seem to be losing them."

You who possess the relevant skills, have been thrown into the dustbin.
You, who gave your all at your own and your family's expense, have been chucked out.
Downsizing, world recession and Covid 19 are taking their toll.
You are out, it is beyond most organisations, and you have unexpectedly joined the unemployed.
You have become a statistic that you never anticipated you would be.
That which you used to hear and see is now right by your door.

In so many phases, joblessness hits hard.
Thoughts of where to start fill your mind and increase worry and anxiety.
Age, outdated skills that do not match new technology seal it all.
Fear of the unknown and fear of being ridiculed squeeze your mind like a vice.
Who will ever look at a CV with such attributes?
That job was a veneer that shielded and covered you.
It took you to dizzy heights where few could match the places you visited.
It pumped you up as you bragged about the high-end schools your children attended.
You showed off the package of your fringe benefits to those working in public offices.
Now all that is no more, the hat you used to wear has been ripped off.
Your ego has been bruised, your confidence and self-esteem are shattered,
Leaving you bare, exposed and vulnerable.
Such is the nexus between joblessness and nakedness

Cheer up; joblessness does not mean the end of you.
Rather, it is the end of a season and the beginning of new beginnings.
Losing that job could be a blessing in disguise as other doors open for you.
So many have gone through the same path and are living better lives than before.
It is time to follow your dream, identify your passion and purpose that can sustain you.

Joblessness sometimes numbs you but at times opens new opportunities you never envisaged.

It requires a positive mind, leap of faith, trust in the man above and all will be well.

Accept that the door is closed.

Hey, do not waste time looking regretfully at it, lest you miss those that are opening for you.

Absent in Your Presence

How could you do this?
Here I am, right in front of you but you act as though I do not exist.
Sometimes your actions are so subtle and at times so glaring.
When I try to talk with you, your eyes are glued to your phone.
Your answers are, "uh" "yeah" "yes" or "no!"
You never give a full sentence and neither do you comment.
How can I be so absent in your presence?

Your silence and facial expressions are so intimidating,
You make it seem like you just do not want to hear anything from me.
Your non-verbal actions make me feel like a small animal ready to be devoured.
You make me feel so threatened and scared even to start a conversation with you.
You make me feel isolated, unloved and unworthy.
How can I be so absent in your presence?

Many times I look back and ask, "How did we get connected?"
Many times I look and ask, "How did I not notice it?"
Many times I look back and wonder where I could have erred.
Many times I look back and blame myself for this new creature that you are.
Many times I have changed my way of doing things but you do not seem to notice.
I have gone out of my way to act and talk in a manner I assumed was respectful,
Still you look at me with disdain and condescension.
How can I be so absent in your presence?

If you did it only to me, I would take it grudgingly.
But, doing the same to your children hurts me to the core.
You have no time for them and are always shrouded.
Time and again they have said they are afraid of you.
Have you ever noticed that the time you come to the living room, they disappear to their rooms?
I have tried to relay this message to you, but you don't seem to get it.
How can you be so absent in their presence?

Josephine Muganiwa

Josephine has written poetry and short stories appearing in various anthologies (*Ghetto Diary, State of the Nation: Contemporary Zimbabwean Poetry*) and projects. She is also a literary critic and has adjudicated numerous literary competitions including NAMA and Cover to Cover.

The Golden Handcuffs

Once upon a time there was an emperor.
He fell out with his servant.
There was no evidence against the servant,
but in his heart of hearts, he knew the servant was guilty.
He loved the servant too much to put him in prison,
so he fastened golden handcuffs on his wrists,
sat him on a beanbag next to him.
The servant still ate what the emperor ate
and dressed in fine clothes.
When the emperor enjoyed his evening stroll,
the servant was by his side inhaling twilight scents.
Word spread of the beautifully engraved golden handcuffs.
Many came from across the world
to admire the emperor's love and mercy,
evident in the servant adorned in golden handcuffs.

Cruelty

Clipping a bird's wings,
Then asking it to fly.

Shades of sleep

I want to sleep a deep dreamless sleep

that rests the body after a long day slogging in the fields.

I want to float on the clouds and reach Cotton Candy mountain,

oblivious of all the trouble on earth.

Sometimes I toss and turn, tormented by the demons that harassed me through the day,

now more vivid in the dream with nowhere to run as no friend can intrude to say hello.

At times I sleep lightly, like a new mother afraid of crushing the newborn soul lying next to her,

afraid of missing that hungry call for milk lest you be labelled negligent.

The worst times are when I close my eyes but the mind continues to add and subtract, fill in puzzles and seek ways out of the maze, to wake up tired and haggard in the morning.

                    If only I could always sleep like a baby!

Paintings

Displayed in an art gallery for all to see, each has a different story to tell; but how many of their admirers know the tale behind each piece, what the artist felt inspired by? Was it a breathless moment with the speed of light or a sleepless night as long as a thousand infinities?

The journey through one's own head, twisting and turning, at times getting lost in the cracks and crevices of memory lane.

Did the artist get so lost, the road became blurred, lines between imagination and reality blended by an unknown force?

Kimberly Mhlanga

Kimberly is passionate about poetry as a way of expressing emotions from various experiences, especially issues to do with grief, love, and heartbreak. She has been writing for a year now and looks forward to establishing herself as an HIV and women's rights activist in the near future. She is part of an online community called allpoetry.com, where she posts some of her poems and tries to perfect her craft through interacting with other poets. Aside from writing, her hobbies include reading self-development books and watching true crime documentaries.

Pieces of Us

I don't want to close my eyes

I don't want to close my eyes because the darkness is my first memory of you

In the dark l reached out, broken and desolate

In desperate need of your warm embrace, desperate need of a lifeline, an anchor

Under the cover of darkness you made me experience foreign tenderness

A new high, my heart beating in sync to yours

Under the night as a blanket, our needs in perfect harmony, l gave in

I poured out my heart and the darkness spoke back

It spoke back in your voice

Claiming me, cradling and holding me

But alas, the same veil of darkness that once was my safe haven has turned into my worst nightmare, taking you from me

Leaving me bereaved

Now that the earth lays on your form

Where shall l lay my head?

I've gone from wanting you to needing you

Nothing else matters...

Dearest Mother

A Nefertiti in your own way
Beautiful big belly, ready to bring forth a new life
Ready to nurture and love
Prepared to give your life in exchange for the one inside you
Without you where would humanity be?
Undiscovered perhaps
Oh beautiful queen!
Are you celebrated enough?

Affliction!

Scared of my demise, I take pill after pill

Scared of opening up, my 'dirty secret' tears at the essence of my being

I take more pills and watch helplessly as I lose a piece of me like a snake shedding its skin except I never get mine back

Melancholy rears her ugly head, bringing morbid thoughts with her

Together, they mercilessly drag me down a bottomless pit

In an attempt to break free I take more pills, but no matter how many of them I pop yesterday's misery is still today's woe

So I decide to stop but alas I slip deeper into the bottomless pit and ever further away from liberation

A Cry for Help

My body, a temple but instead of worshipping it

he criticises every bump and hump,

telling me how he hates the bold stripes on my thighs and bosom and how I would be prettier if I was lighter and skinnier.

He tells me to get rid of this and that, but doesn't he see how confidently I sway those hips?

Doesn't he realise that I'm much more than just a body?

"You are much more than just a body *mtanam* and love shouldn't hurt."

But if that's the case sweet mother, why does my heart tremble with fear at the sight of the man who claims to love me?

Why don't you leave him, my peers would ask.

Looking back, I still have no answer to that question.

Ten years after my encounter with the monster I thought was the love of my life,

I can only say it's our duty as human beings to protect our young girls from violence posing as love.

Women and girls are more than bodies available for pleasuring men.

* *mtanam* is isiNdebele for "my child"

Lin Barrie

Expressing her hopes, fears and love with her paintbrush, her pen, and her palette knife, Lin responds to the world around her. She believes that the essence of a landscape, person or animal can only truly be captured by direct observation.

That exploration, that direct and enquiring gaze, can then grow into meaningful abstraction. Whether as painting, prose or poetry. She states, "I feel an intimate connection with the natural world, ecosystems. From field and life drawings, I create works on canvas, using oils and acrylics. I enjoy the immediacy and abstract quality of my preferred tool, a treasured old palette knife inherited from my father, to create expressive strokes. Much of my painting inspires my poetry, and vice versa!".

After completing a Fine Art Diploma in printmaking, with painting and sculpture, at Durban Art College in 1980, Lin worked as a textile designer, travelling extensively to Europe and the Far East for business and pleasure. In 1991, after returning to Zimbabwe from the Far East, and having explored Chinese brushstroke painting and Indonesian batik techniques, she became a full-time fine artist. In 2010, Lin completed a Creative Writing course mentored by J.M. Coetzee, University of Cape Town. She spends much of her time in the southeast wilderness of Zimbabwe.

Embrace Equity

Equity
is a state of being

Unfettered
by social norms

Released
by uplifting groundswell..

Battered by circumstance,
we are not equal by others' standards
and can never be so,
but we are empowered by sacrifice
individually embraced
given tokens,
granted tickets and passes
to the theatre of LIFE,
each in accordance with our need...

I have dreamed
I have looked to nature and traced tree trunks
I have stared into myself and summoned torsos
I have envisaged the hopefulness
of the hill
of Golgotha—

All Things Connected.

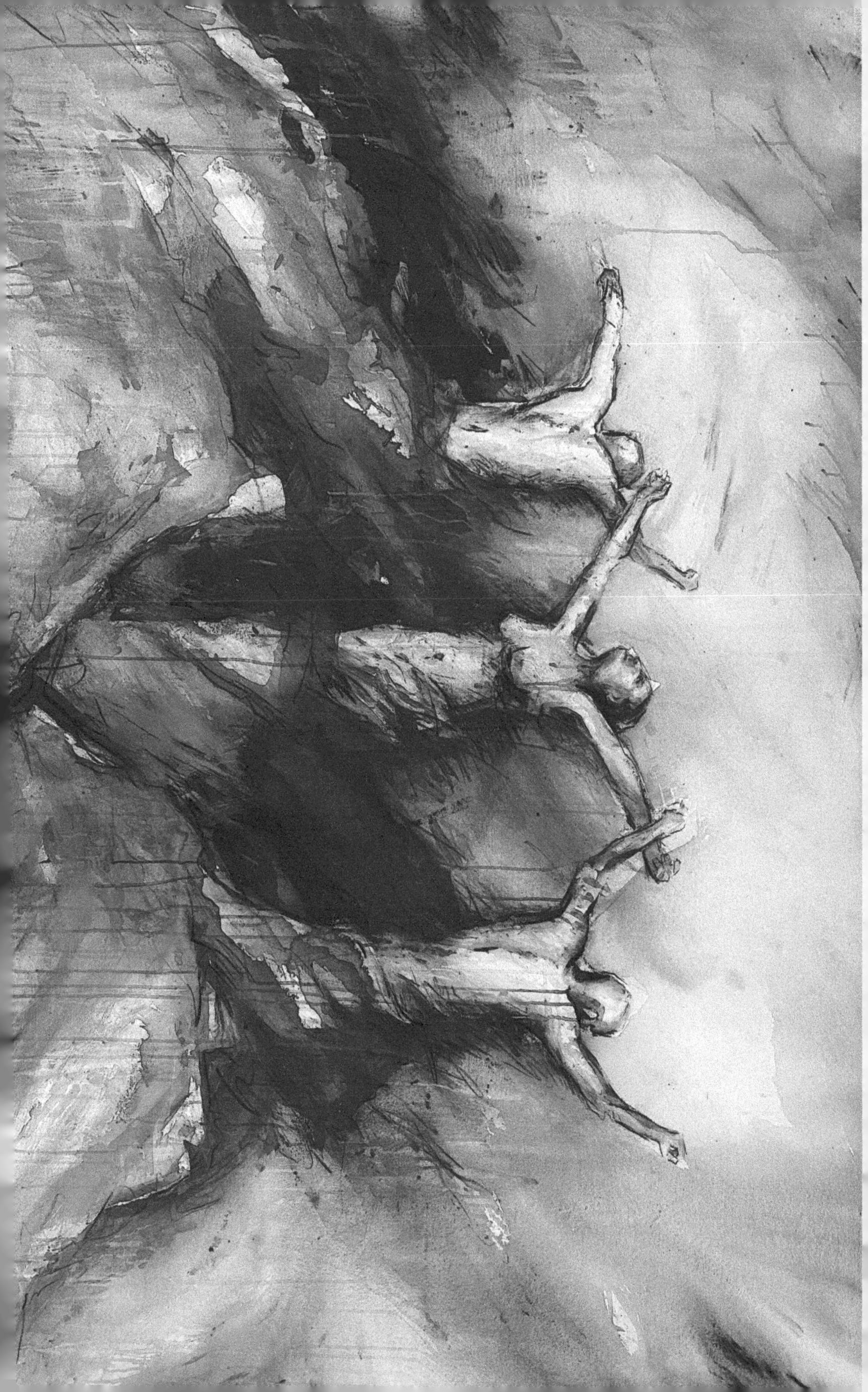

Portrait, taking flight

The power of birds,
wings and things,
is yours.

Close your eyes
tilt your head,
just breathe.

Feel the lift....

Soft feathers tickle tear-tracked cheeks
kind claws scrape hurt from bruised skin
quiet birdsong soothes your ears.

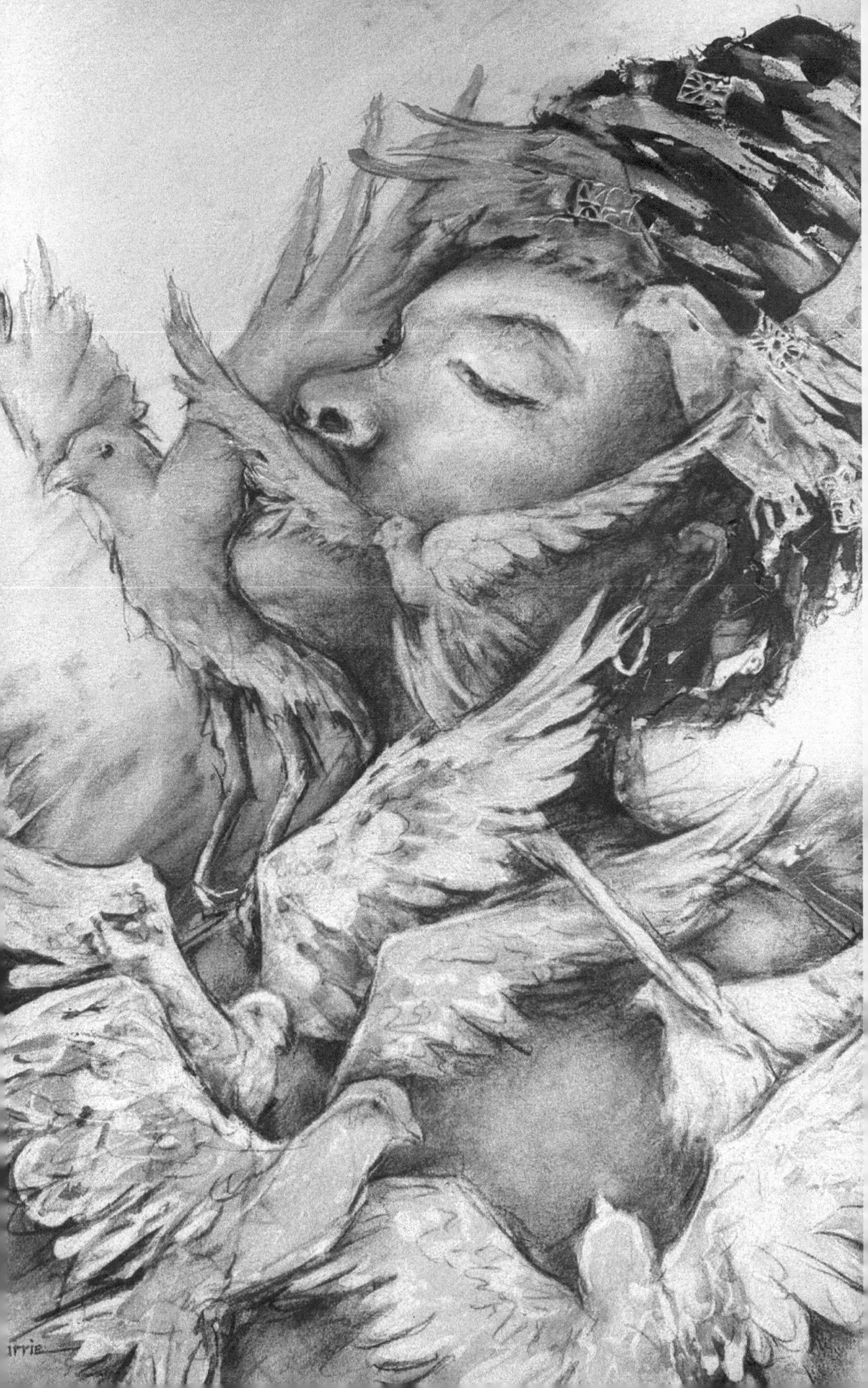

A kite with a broken string has all the sky

A kite with a broken string has all the sky,
no constraint, no boundaries—
a pass to freedom,
flight, adventure.

To Life.

The broken strings in our lives
may seem ill ordained,
untimely,
unsettling,
and yet those same broken strings free us.

We fly from ourselves
to ourselves
in ways unimagined,
unlooked for,
and ever more precious
as we float free.

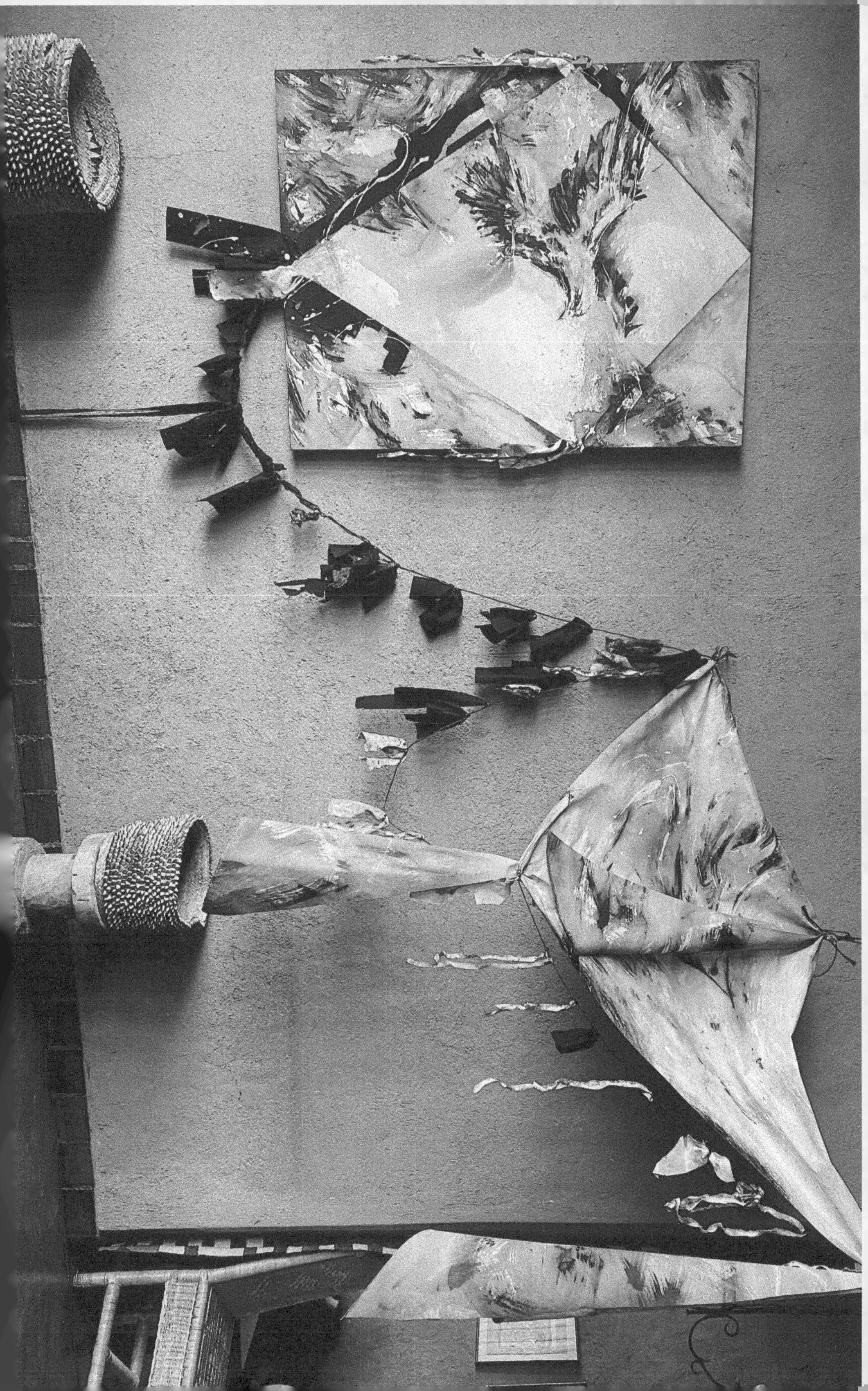

Water

Water is gentle, a cleansing element,
soothing and meditative, but you can drown in it...

Without water
we desiccate,
shrivel and shrink,
body and soul.

But...
dive too deep,
swim too far,
why not?!

Allow the seductive swirls
to pillow your heavy head,
to bury your scoured soul
in eddies of easefulness.

Beware
how you embrace this liquid lushness
this gentle cleansing
this soothing meditation...
you could drown in it.

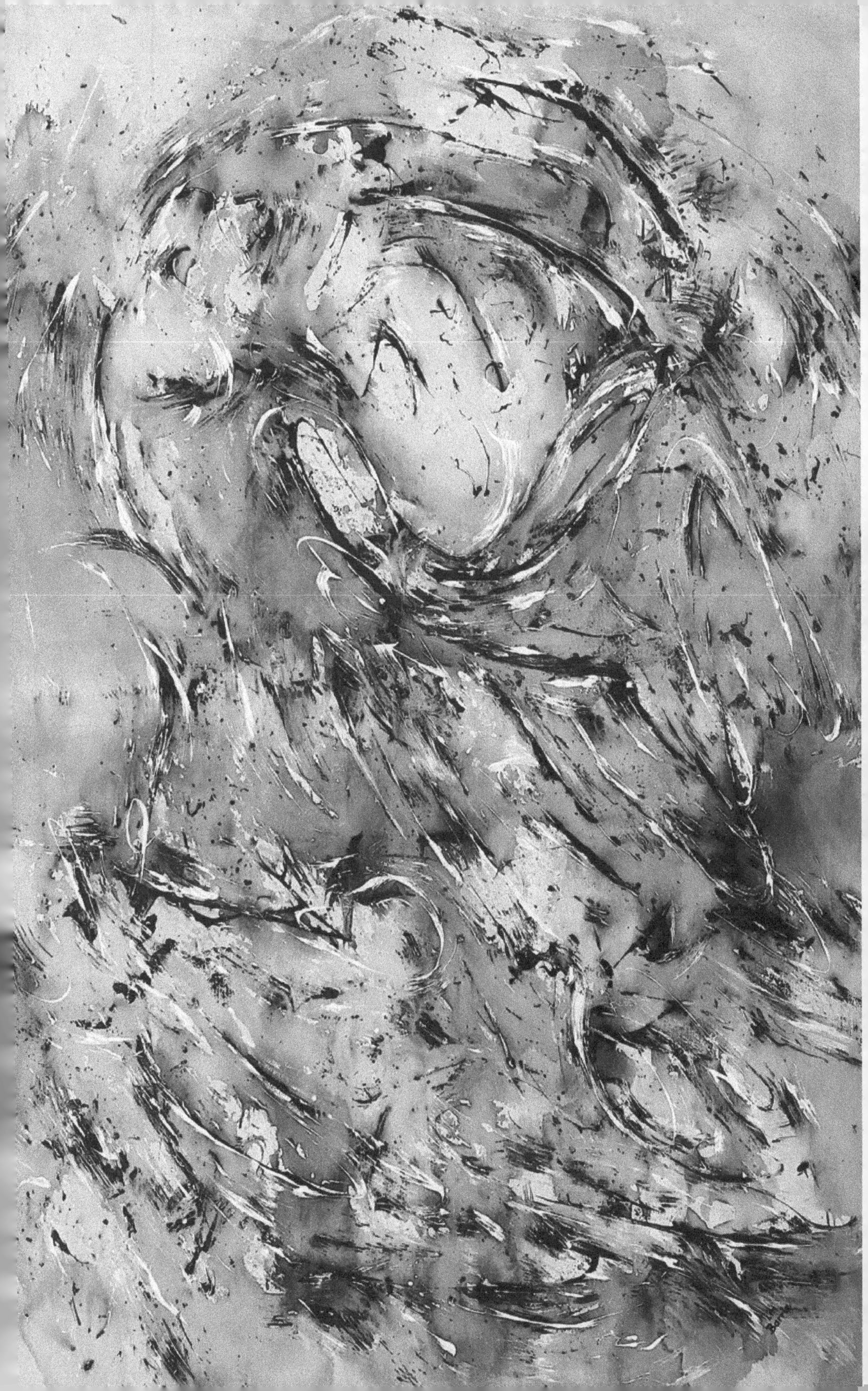

Fire

Fire is fierce, a cleansing element,
creative and turbulent, but you can burn up in it...

Without fire
we shiver,
eat raw,
run wild.

But...
sit too close,
lean too tight,
why not?!

Let the sweet rising smoke
cloud your consciousness,
weave your will
in drifts of warm dreams.

Heed
how you entwine with these flickering flames
these smoky scents
and sizzling sparks...
you could choke in them.

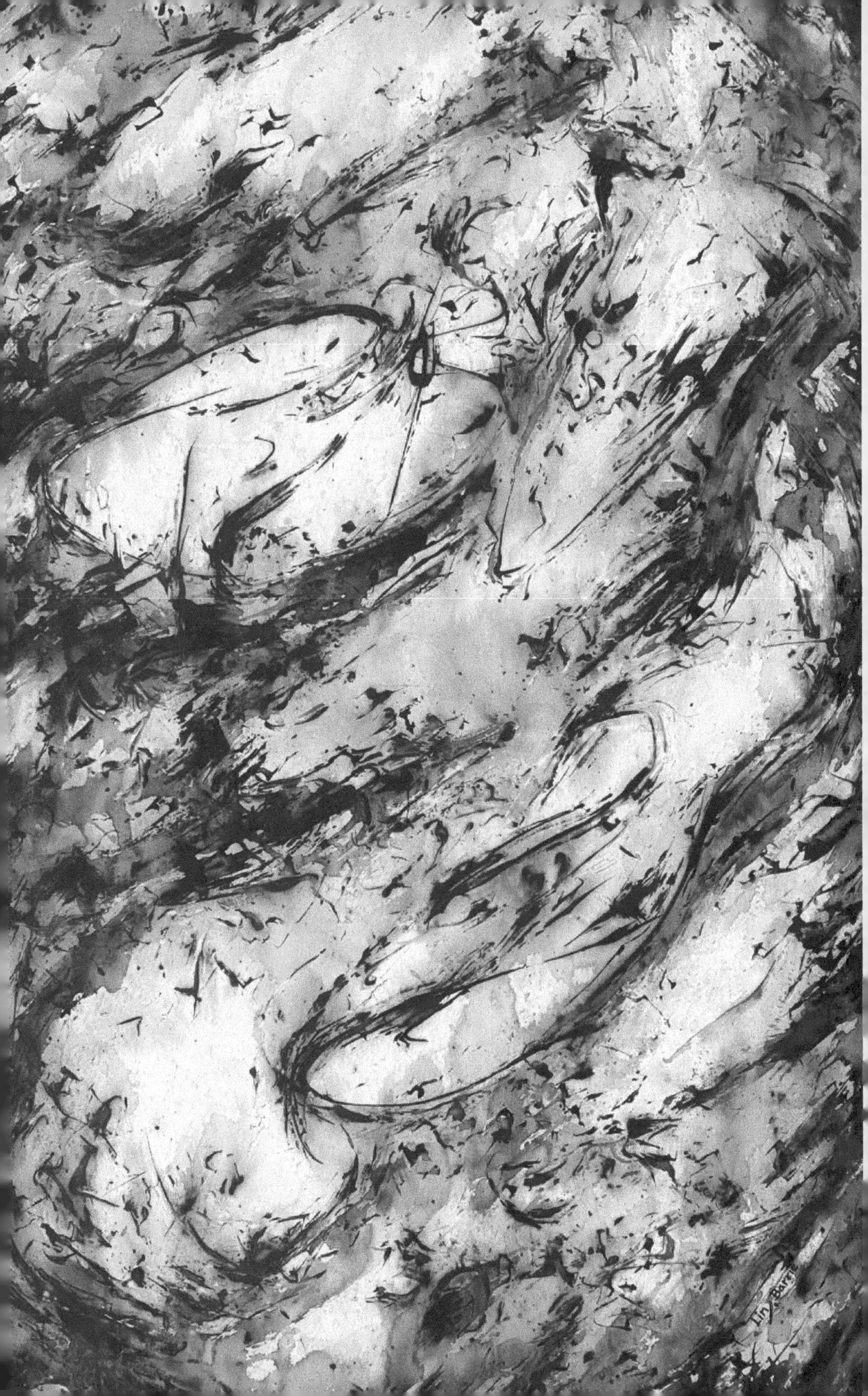

Lucille Sambo

Lucille Sambo is a Zimbabwean born scribe and member of the literati, currently dwelling in and braving the sands of the Kgalagadi in Botswana. Her work has been published in several magazines, including Brittle Paper, Lolwe and Pepper Coast Lit. When she is not pioneering the Afro-punk sci-fi genre, she prefers to immerse herself in the world of Noir Films, Anime, or spend her time in the embrace of the sun.

Wait in the sun

...as far as I remember I had intended on burying her that day, but I found myself sitting on a wooden chair, in a room devoid of all light because to be with her I first had to invite all darkness ever known to man. Right in front of me was what I imagined to be a blank canvas. Time ticked, somewhere, but not in this abyss. Somewhere out there, the earth relentlessly spun on its axis, but there, I floated above all laws of physics. I wanted to conjure one last image of her, but each frame of my mind felt like a cruel joke crafted by the devil himself. I will try again tomorrow I told myself.

*

My world was shaken by the sound of a love leaving me, and each time I try to salvage what is left of her, she crawls out of my canvas, leaving trails of wet paint. Lord knows how many times I have tried to pin her down, but I have grown weary of tracing her & stroking her back together, but the thought of her drying up into stone keeps propelling me forward. Standing on her grave I listen to her softly whisper to me that she needs rest. In the wind, I hold her remains. Today I will bury you, I say, but I forget those words and take her ghost home with me. What kind of love chooses a grave? What happens to the ghosts of people we once loved? What happens when the one whose world yours used to revolve around suddenly ceases to exist? Some find other planets habitable enough for their love, and some just cease to exist completely, but I choose to wait in the sun with a paintbrush in my hand, and here I hope she returns.

R(restricted)

                              The girl
Looks forward to it already
The quintessential effete asshole
That is her father,
& the scissors that snapped her moral fibre
Their house is no different
From a hospital's sickness galore
                              At night,
She fantasises about brilliant paper,
A junky manservant serving the best of grade,
Her fingers crushing each seed of wretch,
Heaping it, misery on top of misery,
Letting the poison squirt into her blood to
jizz on her imagination &
When it finally hits,
The sensation itself
Beats any cock incoculation
It's hardly a substitute though 'cause
The peace it offers is merely a blip
To an otherwise downward trajectory
                              She knows,
But her surgical saw now looks more attractive
She gets a kick from the sight of his corpse
Yanked from the hospital bed with a dissected torso,
The blade slashing through eons of existence,
skewed by a sword, held upward,
hailed & given as a peace offering to the gods,
a white flag drenched with blood, for
to be a true presbyterian she has to stand
underneath her creator(s)
                              "done with this junk"
Yeah, but the shit is never done with her
As long as it has her mother
A long night lies ahead every night
Oh yes it lies, to her behind her purulent brain,

Just one more hit
Because all the fresh air doesn't fucking help either, so
To fix things
She waits for the last thud until
                              She falls asleep.

Waning Gibbous

when a fire stops burning, a woman stands beneath the twilight sky, as she waits for the moon to wane

like a dragon's mouth, she too has to bear the infernal horizons abandoning her, dusk after day, everyday

the feeling returns to her at the speed of the light she has never seen

in the dead of the night, she's the only one awake with the many that have died inside her

many demons she hoards in her womb as she walks with her head scraping the sky, to be she has to be all

when fire stops burning, she leaves the darkness behind her, diving further into the void, the only light

being from the stars that look down on her, spitting on her inflated ego,

reminding her that she is a mere mortal in the face of eternity

the god within her that took its last breath, catalytic to the metamorphosis of her into a shell of herself

the night is not silent; she is the silent one amidst the blaring sirens, distant screams, violent laughter,

and dreams falling from the sky in the form of rain, crashing back onto the earth germinating no seed

a paragon of clitoral massacre, treasure lost, forlorn, scorned, a grave where demons come to feast,

her own freedom fleeting with each rising sun, a vessel rolling endlessly, empty but not without soul,

hers has been replaced by the many who now serpent & dwell within her, trading her insides for hellions

all she has to do to forget reality is allow them back inside, replicating her sores on her lovers,

merging of ancient spirits, most who died a long time ago, and some who are yet to die she gloats over their feeble attempts to resist, like creeping maggots to the stench of death

in the dead of the night, she seems to be the only enlightened one, amidst the rot around her,

further in the dark, she hears the screams of her own shattered dreams, finds them & with them she wails

tantric goddess, an impetus, for if demons are to multiply, they first must have known a uterus

the place of innocence long lost, death is now required for her rebirth

on the most terrible of nights, she surges forward into the storm, using turbulence to propel herself forward,

calm at sea, but cocooned by rage, hers is a life of freedom, so long as it's compromised,

holding back the tide with a broom

the remnant of the conflagration is a woman who has been reborn from the ashes

and yet another one who longs to have perished with the fire's dying embers

Fog

(I)

I heard that snakes open their mouths to invite flies
& because they are attracted to death, they flutter in their lots
because of the scent   no, actually
it's neither a scent nor a smell
it's a particular thing one can't ignore
                                       like a venus plant
has them speculating as to why & how a plant
with leaves & a deep root system in the earth would choose meat as
                                                         its source of survival

(II)

I wear a man's t-shirt and briefs
only the pusillanimous &
                                                         timorous can catwalk
but today I'm unfazed
         I transform my room into a runway
& my full-length mirror into a witness;
                 it attests to my well-defined biceps and perfectly sculpted obliques

(III)

hailing from a place
     where girls are taught to sleep with one tit out, "cause men become thirsty during the
                 night vigil" & clits concealed when men go to war
I also habitually sit with my legs apart
they become moist when they detect a man
                                                                 nearby
occasionally,   I boost my ego with knee-highs

(IV)

want to know what a man loves the most
?   it's a pussy that can sleep in the trash today and also be worshipped the
following day
                                               but what defines a woman's straight?
is it the   forcefully engraved orifice

in between or what they allow   into their mouth?
within mine is saliva that transforms into a vortex of truth whenever I'm confronted
however,   it quickly evaporates when I'm put on the spot

(V)

the airwaves proclaim
that
penises
are for women   &   phalluses are only for females|
         armed with a map, I head towards the chicken coop, upon arriving   it has been
                                                       transformed into an abattoir
there is blood everywhere   from wombs| necks

(VI)

I meet a girl on my journey back
she tells me that my pussy is a trap
for rodents   & that if I don't want it to turn into a crime scene
I have to close my legs or|
—get rid of the cheese
            I tell her I don't want to fuck   I just want to know it's possible

(VII)

on a pillow drenched with tears, she promises me that I don't have to
                          rearrange my particles &
                              physiology
for her to stay
                because there's more to life than constant strife
she says
                she just wants to die having known true silence
tonight   she holds me close & lets me narrate to her the |
story behind the briefs

(VIII)

when I wake up,
she is headless

(IX)

'cause for me to live, something like her|

                                                    has to die everyday

the carnage endures the note;|

(X)

'long as girls don drag
&
boys strum guitars

Mistle thrush

From afar, her requiem echoed/
A mistle thrush with broken wings/
Painted with filth and soil; drawn by tortures and pains/
But her beauty swiftly entrapped me

I administered to her, nursed her/
With my attention, love and compassion/
Gentle and rapid, her recovery commenced/
My survival soon depended upon hers

Eventually/ she started to speak, laugh, cry with me/
Whatever I did, she was by my side/
Took her with me, no matter where I travelled/
My entire life I wanted woven onto hers

Alas! the shining bird got stronger and desired to soar again/
The fear to lose her injected me with grief/
With rage, I built a cage of blood/
And surrounded her

In her cell the bird shut herself off more and more/
To cry, laugh, speak became hard for her/
Death to her missing joy,/
We became two foreign beings, only united in sadness

I opened the cell, regarded my wings/
Painted with filth and soil; drawn with tortures and pains/ For one last time I throw a glance, with a lovely garment she faded into the void/
But I only catch a sight of the neglection of my own soul

Marian Christie

Marian was born in Harare and completed her school education there. She lived and worked in various countries in Africa, Europe, and the Middle East before moving to her present home in southeast England. Passionate about both the arts and the sciences, she holds Master's degrees in Applied Mathematics and Creative Writing, and often interweaves mathematical structures or imagery in her poetry. Her work has been widely published in online journals and print anthologies. She has written two poetry books, *Fractal Poems* and *Triangles* (both published by Penteract Press), and a collection of essays, *From Fibs to Fractals: exploring mathematical forms in poetry* (Available from Ice Floe Press).

When not writing or reading poetry, Marian looks at the stars, puzzles over the laws of physics, listens to birdsong and crochets. She blogs at www.marianchristiepoetry.net

Turbulence

Upstream in pools where the water barely flowed but for a gentle kissing

of the rocks, a tremor in the mirrored clouds – water transparent as air, sprung

from the mountain's flank, too cold for bilharzia-bearing snails –

we found a duiker

its hide beginning to flake, its eyes glazed,

its legs stiff. We tensed too, my brothers and I,

in the cold shock of our discovery. I had not known

death before. Not this close. This unexplained.

The sun's heat bounced off the rocks, drew out the fragrance of the grass. Death

did not belong here. *Take its legs.*

Our feet slipping on riverbed pebbles, we dragged the duiker through the pools

to where the stream began to quicken, to leap over hidden rocks,

swirl in eddies against the banks. Near the precipice

the river's tug became too strong and we released the carcase to the current.

It floated haphazardly, tiny hooves bumping

against water and sky. We ran along the bank

to where the river abandoned all containment and hurled

down a vastness of rock. The duiker disappeared

in that foaming plunge towards the mist-green Honde valley. Above us,

white-necked ravens rode rollercoasters of air.

Daffodils
for my mother

Forty years to the day after you died
I plant daffodils in foreign earth.
You would have rebuked me
for planting them so late,
December already, beneath
frowning northern clouds—
you, who were always late for everything
except, that day, your flight.

lines

contemplate
a world without lines

without fixed points
of beginnings and endings

a soft blur of colour
that has no form

the way light blends with clouds
as earth turns

or the ocean shifts
and shimmers

waves surging
          falling
embracing
          dissolving

consider
how we might

hold only to movement
let our thoughts

murmur like starlings
in autumn dusk

for when we look to the sky
there are
      no
          lines

Citizen of nowhere

He looked at me across the counter, pen poised above the form, and asked where I was born. We had made good progress up till then. Name, age, gender, marital status, I knew all the answers. But now: where *was* I born? A silence floated in the ice-white hall and wobbled outwards like a slowly blown bubble. My breath was going nowhere. He asked again – *Your place of birth?* – and the walls dissolved into sunlight, straggled poinsettia bleeding white, mealies roasted in mopane embers, crack of musasa pods curled beneath my foot. *Somewhere in a non-existent country.* He was getting impatient, I could see, so I wrapped my coat around my self and scrabbled to release my breath. In my mental fists I held two names, one in the past and one in the present. Which one should I give him? I opened my mouth and offered the name that was on the palm of my tongue.

Because no matter how hard I try, I don't understand the rules

I open the door
                a pebble falls

from the puckered mouth
                        of a daffodil

thuds in a flutter
                    of autumn leaves

upends the roots
                  of shattered trees

tilts the earth
                south flips north

sun rises
            from a western sea

tides reverse
              moon spins away

clouds, untethered,
                  flit the sky

where stars fall upwards
                      and explode

pretend you didn't hear me
pretend I didn't speak
pretend my door stayed closed

And for the rest of time

I

don't

recall

my falling.

One moment I was

standing at the edge, admiring

the view – then my foot must have slipped
                        on the age-smoothed rock

                        I tumbled
                                into the ravine

                        helpless
                              fragmented

                        and
                           alone

                            with
                            no

                               way
                                out

Mercy Dhliwayo

Mercy is a creative writer, poet, and hip-hop artist who goes by the stage name Sista X. A human rights advocate at heart, she uses her art as a form of advocacy. Her poetry and short fiction have been featured in local, regional, and international publications such as Karavan Magazine, East Jasmine Review, New Contrast, FEMRITE's *Nothing to see here*, Poetry Potion, and Mosi Oa Tunya Review, amongst others. Her debut short story collection, *Bringing Us Back* was the recipient of the 2022 Zimbabwean National Art Merit Award for Outstanding First Creative Published Work. In 2019 she released her debut hip-hop and spoken word album, *The X A-Gender*.

Dhliwayo is also the founding member of the Slam Emporium Polokwane, an organization that grants a platform for performance and creative growth in Polokwane and its surrounding areas. She has performed in Sweden, Uganda and on various stages in Zimbabwe and South Africa, including festivals such as Poetry Africa International Poetry Festival, Polokwane Literary Fair, and the Intwasa Festival, amongst others.

Facebook: @Mercy Dhliwayo (Sista X)
Instagram: @mercydhliwayo

Cycles

I am slowly becoming my mother
Her sisters
Me: here
Squeezing my feet into their worn-out shoes
Attempting to convince you of the innocence
Of my hand making contact with the menu at the same time as the waiter's hand
Me: Attempting to dissociate myself
from the over-friendly taxi driver and his inappropriate remarks
Me: Apologising for my foot accidentally touching another man's foot
Me: Defending old friendships that predated my acquaintance with you
Me: Not realising that the problem is me; not you
Me: Absorbing your touch like erasure
Numbing the pain with the comfort of your lips
Drawing hope out of your smile and laughter
Hoping your insecurities would not grow into clenched fists
Or land on my face or bruise my eyes
Me: hoping you will change and never grow into my father
All the while
Slowly turning into my mother
And her sisters
Whom I used to question why they never left.

Dear Black Man

    Teach us
           How to write
                  Better poems
                          Of black fathers:
                                    Smiling Poems.

Childhood Paintings

He had his own kind of truth
A collection of paint brushes
Thick strokes painting her evil
And him religiously right
You see, he was always right
Even when the abstract of his art
Tainted him wrong
He just had to be right
Strapping bombs on his tongue
Some kind of jihad
Casualties: the usual suspects
And the collection of artworks
In this museum
Are all too painful memories of childhood.

The Weight of our Fathers' Names

When the new teacher asks for his name
He makes sure to say his name right
Makes sure to correct the Teacher
When he repeats it wrong
The way he corrects the other boys
Who call him wrong
Or grown folks
Who call him something else other than his name
        Like: Boy or Fana or Sonny
He says a firm: No;
        That is not my name
Then he says his name; one more time
First and last name together
Never forgetting the last
His tongue wears his last name firm
As if to assert belonging
He wears his last name with pride
The pride of one
Who does not yet know
The weight of his name
Or the pain of being saddled
With last names
That are often the only things that remain
When daddies forget what they left behind.

Jacaranda

The jacarandas crushing beneath my feet:
Their purple soiled in the mud from last night's rain
Somehow remind me of you.

The petals of your youth
Fragile in their purple hue
Drained of their fragrance and
Replaced with that defiled stench of rot
That follows you when you walk the streets
After a night of boozing
And stranger's semen oozing down your thighs.

Your jaded eyes
Cannot recognise
The dissolute destitute
That has found refuge
In the mirror's reflection of you.

Dejected, you puke
A concoction of ill choices
Laced with fragments of dreams deferred
Muddled in the puddle of heavy rains
Leaving you crushed and muddied
By the many feet
That you have let trample over your petals
And your tired body trembles
Under the weight of these heavy feet
As you repeat familiar rituals
To secure your next fix.

Though jacaranda petals
Fall and lose their splendour
With each foot that crushes them into the mud
From the previous night's rain,
They blossom again with each spring.

But you are no jacaranda
No spring can bring back to life
The blossom and hue
Of your soiled youth.

Nyasha Celeste Makombe

Nyasha Celeste Makombe (who also writes as Thee Poetic Raindrop) sails through the oceans of pen and paper in which she has achieved many successes. Her works have been featured in several anthologies, as well as numerous magazines and newspapers. *Ask my father*, *Paidamoyo*, *Mudzimu ndiringe* and *Tiva ta wena* are her upcoming novels to look out for, accompanied by a poetry book titled *Poetic Raindrops*. To her, poetry is more than putting words on paper – it's about telling stories untold and giving a voice to the voiceless. It is within her soul; the everlasting fire burns.

I write

I write not for fame nor accolades
I write not with ink nor paper
I write not what you want to read
I don't write for you
I write for me

I write with my thoughts and emotions scattered all over the place
I write with tears in my eyes and a heavy heart
I write to silence the voices in my head
I write to numb the pain in my heart
I write to escape this poisoned earth
I write to free myself from your claws
I write to rub off the venom you emit
I write to mourn the child I never got to meet
I write to stay afloat in this raging sea
I don't write for you
I write for me

Spare me your validation I need it not
Spare me those praises I hear them not
Spare me those prizes for they are nothing but heavy ornaments
Next time you read what I wrote
Know that I write but not for you

Lend me a rope

Lend me a rope please
I can't harbour this emptiness any longer
I tried the pills they found me too soon
Drained them out
My key out of this misery
I tried jumping into a river
She caught me, held me, told me this is my home thus I can't drown in water
She looked nothing like an archetypal mermaid
But she was perfect her body cold as winter snow
Held my hand left me by the shoreline
Damn! another escape ruined

I tried to have it my way with a razor blade
It worked I felt my soul levitate
I was free, happy and content
Until I woke up to a medicinal stench
I'm in the hospital again!
Maybe I celebrated too soon
These drips attached to my body are dragging me back

Lend me a rope
For the one behind our kitchen door is far from reach
My Synodia, every time I look into her eyes
I feel guilty I tried to sneak out and hang myself
like the olden days when they made Christmas trees out of people of colour

The look in her eyes tells me if I die she'll follow me without a doubt
I seem to be all that she has
I lost mine, the only fruit my womb would ever bear, four winters back
I don't know what hurts more losing Ntsakelo a child I never met
Or knowing that's the only child I'd ever have
Lend me a rope it probably wouldn't hurt
As much as the pain my soul endures with every breath

Lend me a rope it seems to be the only key out of these woods stenched with darkness
My Synodia, my heart breaks a little when I hear her name
She seems to be the only thing there is to live for
Lend me a rope I will carry it with me just in case the Soul Reaper locates her
I wanna go with her she can't leave me behind
She's the only reason I'm still holding on

Lend me a rope

Mirror

I'm looking through you
Searching for the unknown
Not certain if it's me staring back
But I can surely see my reflection
Eyes blue-black from all the taboos I've seen
Lips swollen from all the lies told
Body fragile a heartbeat away from giving up
Heart dysfunctional, shattered beyond measure
Spirit scared from the vicious attacks that were meant to destroy my soul
All my limbs broken, all my joints dislocated
I knock once, twice
Hello who's there
I know not who you are just a reflection
Those hopeless eyes that seem to have seen it all have become skewed
That unsavoury soul coated in rust seems out of tune
Engrossed in feeding the ego drained, dismantled, tarnished
I chide the lady for letting the venom of the world overshadow her light
Succumbed to unhappiness that birthed to nothingness
I watch in horror as the mirror exposes all that is hidden from the world
Sadness

Should I return

Should I return
To the walls tainted with blood
Floors polished with tears
Rooms roofed with pain
Verandas infested with terror
Air poisoned with hatred
Windows tinted with fear

Should I return
To the one who left me to die in the deserted woods
The Predator that feasts on my weaknesses
The monster who forcefully disbanded my being
The parasite sucking life out of me
The creature with sinister motives planted and watered for me

Should I return
To the tarnished and dusty marriage
To the promises of a better tomorrow
Love coated with unsavoury lies
Being hospitalised in tow
Should I succumb to the fear of a failed marriage?

Nyasha Norah Mavhu

Nyasha describes her motivation for writing as follows:
"My dear grandma did not further her education; she couldn't go to secondary school but she was educated enough to let children be children. She was willing to be called crazy for literally fighting off men. Growing up, I couldn't see why my grandma liked fighting, especially fighting with men when you're a lady! Now I understand she couldn't petition against child marriages and abuse, but in her own way she made herself heard and stood her ground, and was nicknamed 'the undertaker' for her fighting expertise. This is something we have failed to do for those few girls from our homesteads that we know, the stories we have heard, because we thought it's too political, it will ruin relationships in our rural homes or maybe it's because it hasn't or it didn't happen to us! For this reason, I became a philanthropist, the Founder of Falcon Love Trust. It's not about being in a huge organisation, it's my voice being heard. On platforms where people actually care, on platforms where some people are in a capacity to act when my words evoke them to action. And to this journey, humanitarian work through poetry! To letting out thoughts and the truth that no one wants to talk about! Speech bravery! To grandma's legacy! I haven't done much but I was here! I lived! I loved! I did, I have done everything I wanted, and I'll leave my mark, a mark of grandma legacy. To be a carer. R.I.P. Grandma Connie, you would have liked this, like you always said 'kura uite kasikana kakafunda, kakarhwe mabhuku, nekutaure chingezi, kachikwire ndenge!' ('grow into a learned girl child that consumed books, can speak English and fly in aeroplanes!')."

Diluted

What if we not holy but actually behind?
What if we really living in ages behind?
Behind all the knowledge and wisdom
Behind, that sexuality is really a spectrum
What if it's not a sin to be gay like we are told?
What if it's actually natural and God approves?
Our perspective like they say,
Dull, like they say,
The motherland primitive like they say.
What if we need the real revelation from God himself?
That men or women makes no difference.
Then many would have died for no reason,
Been jailed for no reason,
Tormented for how they were biologically made
Discriminated for who they are,
Then we would be doomed, thinking we know better than the rest of the world.
But what if it's the rest of the world wrong?
The world gonna burn in hell!
What if being gay is a sin after all?
Then who is going to save the rest of the world?
Just what if?

The Cursed One

He sees what no one sees
He hears his own things
It's clearer to him and blurry to everyone
The curse I am on!
To notice the priest fondling the maiden.
The neighbours put on fake smiles after the huge fight at night.
A curse it is, to know that some people benefit from child marriages
How the rich gain from the poor in the name of capitalism.
A curse it is, to know no one really helps you unless it's to their advantage
To see mothers exploit their own kids for bread
It's a curse, to know the world is never really gonna change
To know people have died for trying to make a change
It's a curse, to know we're all gonna die,
And the world will remain the same: unmoved!

Long Gone

It's the taste of vinegar and honey
A concoction of mouthwash and alcohol
But the perfect combination of bread and butter
An unhealthy obsession
The heart and soul rhythm
The right pursuit for madness
Cannot be told its obvious foolishness
No wits can grasp how this all forms
Sweat and tears!
The fondling of breasts and thrusts
Real passion and desire
Agony!
My perfect relationship with a drug abuser
His heart full of love, next he is so ruthless
The hieroglyphs on his skin illegible
They take different shapes, I cannot keep up
With you I become so dull and malleable
I will take my chances with you!

The Greed in Me

On the upside down
Taken to the depths of despair
My soul filled with greed
The greed in me takes me to the salty seas
Flying me to uncontentious deserts
Take me to the horizon
Let me watch the sun go down
Take away what I think I love
The posh cars, heaps of clothes and fame
The Instagram likes, Facebook reposts, an influencer!
Take me back to when I needed no one to be happy
When retail therapy was not an addiction
Take me back to when family cared for me
It's a price to pay
You got a price to pay!
In my own race,
I need more, I need everything bigger and more visible
I need to be better than everyone, enslaved by my own greed
When they get a hundred, I want thousands
When they travel around the world I wanna go to space
I want more than they have
To be a social media sensation
To be in the spotlight
To be the G.O.A.T.
What I need is to be the undefeated
What happened to me?
It's a blessing and a curse
At whatever cost there's a greed in me
An insatiable quest for what cannot be found
To be happier than everyone else!

Patience Tinotenda Mutsetse

Patie is a passionate social worker with a Bachelor of Social Work Honours Degree from the University of Zimbabwe. She is a feminist leader, creating safe spaces for women to engage in transformational conversations, and a feminist writer whose work has been published in Open Democracy, The Spill Mag and Essence Girls United. Her areas of expertise include women's rights issues such as Gender Equality, Feminist Leadership, SRH, SGBV, FGM Menstrual Health, and Climate Change. She is a spoken word performer and multi award winning poet whose work has featured in Tsonga Mukololo Publications (One Project), Vasikana Project (Menstrual Health Poetry Competition) and YouthHubAfrica (Youth Voices on Ending FGM). She is a digital storyteller with a personal blog called Her Diary Conversations. She is also a member of Women's Coalition Zimbabwe and Amnesty International Zimbabwe (AIZ). Patie is a 2023 AIZ #YouthPowerAction fellow.

How Our Fathers Break Our Hearts

Then, there comes a time
When the grooming hooks our minds
With our mothers' habits we become stuck for life
Before the alarm goes off
We swiftly leap out of bed and kneel beside our beds
An Amen to conclude our devotions shift our minds to cleaning
Accidentally or coincidentally we bump into each other in the passage
Our hands touch as we both try to reach for the garbage

We suddenly catch sight of their baggy black eyes
For a moment, the whole world stands still
And finally with a shaking and pained voice
The most inappropriate greeting slowly slips from our mouth
Mangwanani amai

There comes a time
When our mothers cannot conceal the bruises anymore
Whether we have become old enough to notice the abuse
Or they have become exhausted enough not to hide their pain
Whether they have stopped their morning facial routines or
We have started to roam around before they have pampered their faces
The reality remains the same
We begin to question our fathers' characters

Our respect for that one person
We had grown to embrace as our protector starts to wither
In place of love, hurt is stamped
In place of honour, resentment grows
We begin to blame ourselves
For not being sensible enough to realise that
Those we are proud to call our fathers are the worst monsters
And this is how our fathers break our hearts

* *Mangwanani amai* is Shona for 'Good morning, mother'.

Silencing my Voice

Silence is the hot flashes of anger
I block from erupting out of my mouth
Silence is the thunderous voice
I block from escaping out of my mind
Silence is the pool of opinions
I block from evaporating out of my heart

I keep hopes, aspirations and prayers
Close to that only place I trust
At birth I was told to hush
At five I was told to behave
At twelve I was told to grow up
At sixteen I was told to know my place as a woman
All in the name of silencing my voice

Buried Deep Within Us

Buried deep within us are the untold stories of our grandmothers
The stories that never escaped the bearers' hearts
The stories that lingered in their minds until death called them home
The stories that could start revolutions
The stories that could finally break their silence on intergenerational trauma
The stories that were nicely folded and tucked into shelves
Only accessed through personal, deep and intimate conversations by the fire.

Placed on our backs are rich graves of our mothers' ideas
The thought-provoking ideas that were never published in books
The meaningful opinions that could change the world
We carry within us
The inspirational quotes personified by idioms and proverbs.
Maybe if our mothers could read and write
Our libraries would be fully packed with more stories of home
Stories that we could relate to.

Heavy on our hearts is the burden of our own lived experiences
The stories of love, passion, hope, faith, success, personal growth and feminism
The stories of migration, betrayal, loss, grief, depression, trauma, anxiety and disappointments.
These are the narratives we lock in our hearts
The hidden stories that weigh on our minds
But we can never keep history alive by being silent
We can only keep it alive by allowing the fire within us to explode
Our history as African women is safe only if we share our stories
We can freely paint our worlds with words.

We need to honour the generation of our daughters
With more stories of our realities
Stories that reflect our heritage, our identity, our pride
Stories that reveal our soft spots, our struggles and our victories.
We owe it to our daughters
To be vulnerable enough to write stories
As manifestation of their heritage, our identity,
Embracing our past and present reality
Our flawed and perfect stories.

Behind

Behind those heart palpitations
there is a story I can't tell.

Emotions,
unstable moods
and feelings of detachment
only point to the story I can't share.

Behind those closed doors
there are loud sobs I suppress.

Hurt,
the scars
and the pain in my eyes
only point to the screams I bottle.

Behind that respected family
there is a monster we protect.

The censored jokes,
laughs and
the silence of my mother
only point to a broken home.

I Have a Habit

before I slide between the sheets
I open my closet
to search for a delivery
the one I was served with some years ago
the one I was forced to sign for

as soon as I lay my hands on this parcel
I quickly unpack its contents
a roughly packaged memoir
with my name printed on it
a memoir that's written for me

with chills all over my body
piercing through my veins
I reluctantly drift away into sleep

even in my dreams
I have a habit
of tolerating nightmares
that disturb my peace

Pauline Chirata Mukondiwa

Pauline is a retired economist and development consultant with a passion for improving peoples' lives. Resilience in people, especially when they are tested by hardships, inspires her. A mother of three adult children and a grandmother of two, she is driven by the marvels in nature, heritage and spirituality. She has published in Shona, novels: *Mhere yeZevezeve* and *Zvinobvinza*. Both talk of heroines who were meant to sink in their circumstances, and be victims but they sailed and became victors. She has also published a collection of poems; *Tsapi yeRurimi Rwaamai* in Shona and *Memories are Forever* in English. Both collections are fun and laughter, serious and reflective, ooze with love, loyalty, pain, partings and grief, subtle rebukes, Zimbabwean life settings, Savannah and tropical sights and sounds. Her 'Ndakazvidengezera', published in Ipikai Poetry Journal, Issue 2, serenaded a Photographic Exhibition at Secession in Vienna, Austria, in February 2023. In her writings, she unapologetically hangs her heart on her sleeve as she showcases her own and others' life experiences.

Universal Usage

Trees and flowers can be planted everywhere
Cleaning detergents work anywhere
Uptown or downtown use anyway
Trails not to replace potholed pathways
Move forward and ahead to non-crater highways
No planning haphazardness...no way
No excuse 'by the way'
No busy ugliness just easy laziness

Full wardrobe or one dress
Wash iron and remove dross
With teeth ... brush and floss
Cut out the bad mouth
No words that are uncouth
No ugliness otherwise its laziness

Urban peri-urban or rural position
High or low-density accommodation
Love with intensity your location
Your very own locality for vacation
Cleanliness is godliness... no reason for frivolity
Location is right here... difference is attitude

Adapt what works there to work here
Pull socks up and roll up those sleeves
Back-to-back back-breaking JOB no backstreet
No justification for dirty ugliness
Nor non-thinking rubber-bones laziness

Love is in it

Grace in being fecund and working
Salty taste of my warm sweat
Its putrid smell from a full day's slogging
Painful tiredness steely sweet
Gaping pocket holes barely patched
Striving and my love being fanned

School runs and car pooling
Homework and me learning
School meets, teacher consultations and activities
Job applications interviews and first day at work
Hand-holding in life's fire-fighting and challenges
Driving and my love embers have a new glow

Baby-sitting ... diapers potty training cartoons
Advice two-way seeking and giving
Financial social and technological quotient
Friends and equals that are different
Prospered partnered protected by womb product
Thriving and my love firing from all cylinders

Looking up and praying to be here for longer
Flourishing and love is the fountain of it all

This too will come to pass

It's only yesterday...
All adults were Brobdingnagian giants
I moved from teated bottles to cups with spouts
I wore my training potty as a hat
My toys were my best friends
Ken and Barbie were the 'couple'
Then... I was 'the boss of me'
Strapped my doll babies on my back
And went 'shopping' with them in my tiny stroller
I put both legs in one leg opening of my shorts
I learnt my arithmetic A B C and to write cursive
I had support wheels on my bike

It's only yesterday...
I stuck to cartoons channel and I hid the remote
I didn't want to bath before bedtime
I swallowed toothpaste 'yoghurt'
I hid from my homework chore
Then... I had imaginary friends
I played until I was tired
balloon stomp... name that tune
scavenger hunt...
G O A T... the plastic stuffed ball

It's only yesterday...
Breezed through junior school to junior high
Senior high made me freeze with 'hardships'
Book piles and deadlines clashing
Those white blazers lapel laden with club and accolade pins
Exams and graduation ushered in university
Then... Wow untethered freedom never seen or imagined
Freshmen weekend spilling into Monday and Tuesday
Sophomore TGIF starting on Thursday
'Doing the owl' and camping in Library third and final year
Graduating cum laude a feat... never mind 'tops'

Love vibes butterflies partied in my stomach
Welcome world and wedding bells

It's only yesterday...
Wedded bliss morphed to 3am bottle feeds
Couple became 3... 4... 5... and auxiliaries ...
the more the merrier... painful truth of significant 'outsiders'
my pseudo utopian marital union bubble bust
eyes opened wide cannot unsee nor ears unhear
Then... I cannot unfeel serious growth spurt and mental nourishment
Age stealthily crept upon me
I am the elderly I saw yesterday
Their aches and pains then are now mine
Natural dystrophic arthritic joints creaking
Slowing everything to robotic graceful motion
Speech oozing eye-witness wisdom and experiential learning
Grey hairs announcing 'I've been there'...

It's only yesterday
I grew... physically emotionally spiritually... and...
I experienced the wealth of... love pain joy loss betrayal and...
My heart's delicate fragility... life's mysteries... I experienced...
This too will come to pass.

Pregnant Rain

Hiding the sun... dark and... threatening
Behind clouds silent and serene multiscreen
Deep grey to light black streaks in between
Cooling thoughts of heat that had been
Clear promise heralded in its sheen
Its menacing goodness unseen
Growth beckoning but unnoticed
Cannot be forever hidden

The heavens split and splatter... tearing
Sky spits letting go its welcome tears
ground swallows and soaks covering chasms and tears
swallowed... vanish wilted plant thirst fears

new bird songs and flora buddings
new skin tones and hair glowing
umbilical cord five-course table servings
invisible growth but visible girth widenings

threatening thunder of silent morning sickness hits
intermittent lighting sharpness of third trimester heat
stepping on the hailstorm of oedema feet
puddles of a Herculean protracted labour feat

rainbow and quiet calm after the storm
labour ward's pleasure of the piercing first cry

Welcome cirrus Cyrus cumulus Claudius
Rain... water table and wetlands pleasure
Blessed beautiful multiplication

Rosemary Chikafa-Chipiro

Rosemary Chikafa-Chipiro is a poet, African feminist, cultural critic and an academic. She is a lecturer at the University of Zimbabwe in the Department of Creative Media and Communication. She is interested in researching and writing about African women. So far, her work has largely been academic and cuts across literature, film and the media. The poems in this collection are her first published poems.

My Butterfly

I saw them,
white and beautiful,
rising from the bushes
with the early morning sun.
White and beautiful.

I squealed with joy,
Children! Children!
Come and see,
white and beautiful
butterflies.

I saw you,
white and beautiful.
I jumped with joy.
Let me catch you,
white and beautiful,
my butterfly.
You flew and flew,
white and beautiful.

The child caught you.
Your white and beautiful wings fell.
I saw you.
Lying there.
My butterfly.
Without your wings...

The Chandeliers in Your Eyes

I wanted to tell you a story
crafted from the sunflowers
I saw in your eyes.
But when I woke up today
I saw chandeliers
hanging from the ceiling,
burning bright in your eyes.
They blinded me
and brought tears to my eyes.
I saw them burning bright
and heard them crash in my head—
The chandeliers in your eyes!

It Was Me

Did you tell her
that it was me who planted the subtle smile on your mouth?
That it was my mouth you teased with your lips today,
or that when I opened the door
you closed it gently behind you
and pulled me towards you,
with your hands teasing the small of my back,
and your lips were always gentle and soft
on my neck?
Did you tell her about how our eyes met,
drunk with desire and knowing smiles,
or that we lay there afterwards, clinging to each other,
afraid that we would lose each other in between,
or that our pillow talk was as naked as our entwined bodies?
O! and the low chuckles.
Did you tell her about how at home you were
in my bosom?
That you were both a man and a child
in my arms,
and that you enjoyed me,
but she was a good woman?
When she said that you look happy,
Did you tell her it was me?

You, Me and the Rain

So, I wanted to write a poem
about you and me
and the rain.
About how I fell for you
on a rainy day
like the rain drops,
drenching you with my wetness,
and you, lapping me up
and sucking me in
like the dry soil.
I wanted to write a poem
about us,
you, me and the rain.
About how we sat
on a rainy day
and you seduced me
with rain talk.
But I cannot write the poem
because I am thinking about
you, me and the rain.
I am watching the rain flow down the pane
like the tears on my cheeks,
blinding me
like your love.
I can only see it,
us,
you, me and the rain.

Rain Talk

Babe,
Today the rain carries my tears for you.
They are lost in the nostalgia of children
opening their mouths
to the pouring heavens,
thirsting but never quenching.
Like I opened myself to you,
many a time.
Receiving you
like the wave hitting the beach.
Teasing, licking,
touching and withdrawing.
Coming and lingering,
but never staying.
Babe,
today the rain leaves me drenched.

Photographer: Wonai Haruperi

Rutendo Chichaya

Rutendo Chichaya is a writer, poet and blogger from Harare, Zimbabwe. Her short story 'Visiting Hour' was a finalist for the Hamwe Short Story Contest in 2021 and 'Herald of the New Times' was shortlisted in the 2020 Intwasa Short Story Prize. Her work has been featured in the following publications: *Ipikai, Intwasa Short Stories Volume One* and *The One Poem Anthology: Survivor's Edition*. Rutendo reviews books on her blog, Rehab and Relapse, which was shortlisted for an AfroBloggers Award in 2021. She is also the host of Ihwi, a podcast that focuses on storytelling. Rutendo is currently working on a collection of poems for publication.

Survival's Spine

33 bones snapped in the wake of dusk
each one of them stood and looked at you in pain.
you asked them, what could it be that gave them so much anguish.
without an answer they looked you in the eye and immediately you knew.

                                                      you
                                                   knew
                                                 because all
                                                 along it
                                                 had been
                                                 you.

one by one you took them into your arms and cradled them.
like a choir under the direction of its master,
each of them, 33 bones in all, sang in your arms, to the sway of your cradle.
how long they'd waited to be in your arms, how long they'd waited for your tenderness to sing to you these words in harmony;

                                     you will not burn yourself,
                you are home.
                                     you will not deform yourself,
                you built this home.
                                   you will not displace yourself,
                you own this home.

there is a life in each letter on which this home is built.
reform the displaced and fill in the gaps with new life
scour the stains of old lovers that compressed you till you crushed your name and buried it in the desert sand.

                                                throw away
                                                the
                                                remnants of
                                                the echoes
                                                of

the butchering of your name.
spit that bitter taste of strange identities that they threw in your face.
you feigned peace and acceptance when you embalmed your name,
keeping appearances but look today the bones stand in truth.
resurrect your name if you wish, forge a new one if you must.

here's what you'll do; you will know your name.
you will call it five thousand times as you face life and it sinks into your reflection.
you will call your name five thousand times and obey your spirit to answer until it is familiar to you like the tongue in your mouth,
      until you cannot do without it,
      until it is a part of you,
      until, until it is the key to your survival.
answer to your name.
repeat it loud and clear, first to yourself and then to others come what may.
quiver and refuse to answer when they mispronounce it.

you see this life? own it.
         break bones, burn bones and bury those bones,
those that no longer serve you any good.
make new bones and piece them together ligament by ligament,
reform, adjust, fill in and move.
you will not carry the burden and
you will not break your back.
         can you hear the sound of your name?
doesn't it feel alive rolling out from your mouth, reflecting from your eyes and sweating from the pores of your skin?
         33 bones snapped in
         the wake of dusk to
         remind you of who you
         are,
before another night of answering to hate
before another day of living a lie.
you are whole.

Dirty Linen

Some poems need to be struck out by a gentle and slow hand.
Of what use are the rhymes and stanzas when time has passed by,
when dreams have dissolved with the fading sun, leaving only
wounds bright and infinite like the stars in the dark blanket of the night?
The wounds cannot be erased, scoured or burnt,
for there is a season that must be accounted for, by blood, sweat or tears.
There is a season, but what use are words that mirror dreams you'd rather leave behind?

Some poems do not deserve to see the light of day.
The questions, mysteries and reflections should lie safe between the traces of memory where no amount of searching, asking and yearning can rewrite what has already been.
Writing the lines, even reading them out loud, feels like hanging linen that you've slept in for far too long, on the washing line where neighbours point and whisper,
"She slept in it for too long."
"Look at that stain it will never come off."
Damning.

The stanzas and sonnets feel like shame,
even when you do what needs to be done.
1. You wash it, no detergent and willpower is enough.
2. You hang it on the washing line already fighting for its life and the edges dangle and sway in the dust.
3. You leave it out to dry for all to see.
Then the fingers point and the voices whisper.

So the shame comes again, and you leave the linen out too long to dry,
counting the hours until nightfall.
But you know that the sun has scorched and stiffened the fabric and everything becomes harder.
You gather enough courage to bring in your linen under the cover of darkness.
No one can see you, but what is there to see really?
All has been revealed and scrutinised.

That is the only linen you own and you refuse to go to bed without it.

It is the only warmth that you now know, the only caress that your body now anticipates; washed, dried and somehow fresh.

Some poems do not deserve to see the light of day.

You hold the edges of the linen with your shaking hands,

the memories and stains in the seams too heavy for the physical and too filthy for the spiritual.

You breathe heavily now only to the rhythm of the air and the fabric swaying in your hands.

You put the linen on the bed and you lay in it ready.

You are used to going to bed naked so your body feels warmth, now oddly familiar, somehow new and then it breaks.

You weep, your body breaks again, this breaking now a reflex.

It breaks again, this time into infinite pieces like the stars in the night because everything feels like hell in the blanket of darkness.

Desires and Burdens

There was a time when I wanted you
in all the parts of my days and the ripples in my laughter.
I wanted you to fill in
     the [spaces]   between my fingers and the vacant parts of my flesh.
I wanted you to colour in
     the [spaces] between my arms and the vacant part between my thighs.
I wanted you to lodge in
     the echoes... behind my voice and the beat in my heart.

There was a time when I wanted you to be my everything.
I gave it to you and you became it all...
...then I wanted to breathe.
               a breath so deep to uproot me from you.
so big to shift shapes of us, snapping me from you,
               so high to sink the high of us, unyoking me from
    you,
so wide to envelope me, insulating me from you.
               I wanted you. You became too much. I wanted
    you.

          Then, I wanted to breathe.

Saturday 5 pm

I walk into the kitchen and the scent of the eucalyptus in my hair fills the room.
pitter-patter, pitter-patter, pitter-patter the soft rain goes on the roof above me.
an empty champagne flute stands in the sink waiting,
you know how I feel.
I am waiting too, soft and light like the rain falling above me.
you know how I feel,
incessant and clear like the rain I can see through the window.
is there something I can cling to,
like the beat in my heart or the pound in my mind?
is there something I can cling to
perhaps, the blend of sharp eucalyptus, acidic bubbly, and the earthiness of wet soil?
is there something I can cling to
like a world of my own and a life full of love?

Home

I bless the tender days where we hold each other in love.
The days when the sun blazes
and the rains still come to cool the wrath of the heat.
The days when the rains pour and
the rainbow appears to console our drenched souls.
Bless the tender days my heart, where amidst all the chaos this love holds its own.
My heart prays for these days when friendship feels like home.

Ruvimbo Martha Jeche

Ruvimbo Martha Jeche is a bilingual poet and short story writer, and a BSc Honours in Administration and Master of Public Administration graduate from the University of Zimbabwe. She writes for all humankind, that is, the man and the woman as a religious specie, psychological/ mental being and importantly as a citizen to be appreciated and included. She advocates for inclusion of the civic and human rights in public policy and governance processes. She has published a poetry collection titled *The Midnight Haul* and is a co-author of *Dear Married Man* and *Jongwe neSheche*. Her work has been featured in The Newsday Zimbabwe, News Hawks, Bold Dialogue Magazine and the Queensdale Report (courtesy of the Gourd of Consciousness Poetry) and in the 2023 International Human Rights Festival *Speaking Truth to Power* poetry anthology.

Silent Prayers

Silent through the storms
I hear a wild voice calling me,
Calm in the deepest winds.
I feel nature embracing every piece of me.
I stop and listen to every thought in me.
I realize I desire the deepest heart
To lead me through my own mind!

Silent prayers I have made,
My voice is no more!
It has been washed down by the thickness of the forest.
A forest similar to my own household,
A household of fists and quarrels!

Maybe this last silent prayer will bring a cry of joy.
Then I will know I was wrong and my elders were correct
When they said:
Heavens search through weary hearts,
They hear silent prayers
And for every soul an answer is certain,
For silent prayers hit heaven with power
And heaven will hit back with miracles unimagined!

Tell Me the Old Story

It's the story of love and peace that brought me up.
Love not known but lived,
Peace not heard but experienced.
The story of warriors who did not give up,
Of intercessors who did not tire,
Of teachers who did not lose heart.
It is a story of a generation that worked so hard,
Believing in the stories of their time!

It's an old story that gave me a hope for tomorrow,
It gave me a reason for being
And for every reason I saw a brighter future ahead.
Now that I'm grown
Childhood stories are gone,
No more bedtime stories.
Grandma is not there to tell me the tales of her time.
From where shall the lessons of hope and future come?
Oh dear mama,
Tell me the old story
Then maybe I can believe again!

Roaring Woman!

Then roaring woman she is,
you say so
but before your appeal,
have you ever thought of
how much she conceals
under her irritating screams?

A roaring woman she is,
you feel so
but before your ordeal,
did you let her feel your love
in her soft-hearted bosom?

A roaring woman she is, yes
she screams when she is burnt,
you should know before you spit at her:
Let her be real,
Hear her
Let her heal,
Love her!

When Lola Left Home

When mother brought her a Barbie doll
Instead of the toy car she wanted,
She screamed out and father shouted at her
And she went to sit in the rain.
Water droplets rolled down her cheeks
She licked them as she began smiling,
She wandered into the forest,
As she heard the chirping birds,
She felt secure,
Happiness she had found.
No one bothered.

The love that burnt in father's house,
She had found
She had seen beyond the dark.
She had wandered into a light,
Unknown.
She was to live her way,
Thinking her absence bothered no one.
But her absence was a torment,
They had to search for her!

I Wanted to Write a Love Poem

I wanted to write a love poem
About the love next door,
But I ended up writing
About how much I hate it with you.
I sang to it,
Word for word,
It sank into my heart
But I erased it from my mouth.
I did not want to give you the satisfaction
That you trouble me
Because of the hurt
You plant into my soft soul.

I wanted to write a love poem.
I smiled into the mirror.
I saw my lips shining
As I pronounced
I love you, Tim!
But looking deeper into my mirrored self,
I recalled the depth of the heartache
And the pity I have for my own life.
I laughed hard as I screamed,
Tim!
I hope I will get better
And write love poems.

Photographer: Annie Greatorex

Samantha Rumbidzai Vazhure

Samantha is a bilingual poet, novelist, librettist, short story and screenplay writer, translator and visual artist who grew up in Masvingo. She resides in Wales, usually writing about matters of the heart, the human condition, the migrant experience, womanhood and equality. She has published a poetry collection in chiKaranga, *Zvadzugwa Musango*, which she translated into English as *Uprooted;* a novel *Painting a Mirage;* and another poetry collection, *Starfish Blossoms,* which won the National Arts Merit Award for Outstanding Poetry Book in 2023. Some of her poems appear in Ipikai Poetry Journal, and her visual art in *Writing Woman Anthology – An anthology of African Asian Writers and Artists Vol.3* published by Mwanaka Media and Publishing. Samantha established an independent press in 2020, Carnelian Heart Publishing, to amplify the voices of Zimbabwean writers. As editor and publisher, Samantha has published various works comprising literary prose and poetry, including two anthologies of short stories by Zimbabwean writers – *Turquoise Dreams* and *Brilliance of Hope*, of which she contributed two short stories to the latter – 'Barcode' and 'Tariro'.

there are no words

for how i feel lying in bed mid-morning, full of fancy and outlandish thoughts, waiting and wanting; my fluttering chest makes me ill at ease about—

                                                         my
                                                        age

and i wonder whether broken older women are allowed to be in love, to be savoured like infusions of luxury loose leaves. does fine tea taste good in crumbling teacups? like

        women

raised by mothers reminded daily that they did not deserve love, no matter how much they gave. like tea sweepings with base flavour, they got nothing but apathy, and tried harder. they were rebels, those women, injecting more and more love into hate 'til they hurt in pendency

i too am a rebel, a different kind, scouring for raw love 'til i feel it frisking in my marrow. for what is life without love? yet, to yearn for it so intensely feels foul, and surreal to feel the wanting returned...

when i think of how much i want to feel your hands on my skin, i quiz my urges—is this love or lust? the probing of feelings ingrained in women shut down to their needs & desires, shamed all their lives for just being. like

                                                        tea
                                                        dust

but i am who i am, lusting...loving...being. when i think of us as one, the depth of expectancy brewing in my soul reboots my mind, a sweet evanescence repeated, again. and again. and again. i'm spent by playing out the scenes of us together, yet my mind won't rest. i try to pen my emotions, but i fail the words

as much as they fail me

Lullaby for a sleepy heart

You have a sleepy heart that doesn't
Remember much about love
And a rigid waist that doesn't
Remember how to move
But when you face your next kiss
The seven archangels hover over you
To sing a lullaby for your sleepy heart
& as your flesh unfurls to their euphony
Your spirit awakens &
Your tongue recalls
      how to dance

Bug of insurgence

The dung beetle thrives on shit

Persistently rolls in mess
It even chooses its mate
Based on the size of its balls... of shit
Then it lays its eggs in those balls of shit
And when the eggs hatch
They eat their way out of it

I ate my way out of shit
Thriving off its nutritious moisture
But hating its stench and hue
The cycle will not be repeated
Nevermore will I roll in indignity
Or flourish in it, for my own sanity
And of those who come after me

What sort of peace...

        does a woman scour for

    at four in the morning?

Other than trying to outrun
    the shadows of her past mistakes
    I can think of one other thing—
    what it means to forgive her evaporating self
    whilst holding on to the human she used to be
    praying for break-neck pace to Godspeed
    to rid throbs caused by ghouls that rob when no one is looking
    like whoever raped that other girl when no one was watching
    then reframed her teenage pregnancy as an immaculate conception.
She feels
        like karma from past lifetimes
        like an imposter
        like holy men's miracles
        making all others seem like they are not of God.
She's a woman being a human no longer being
trying to forgive herself, but like death taking its time
she feels no peace because...
what are mistakes?
        "kupata!" ...*poor choices* that led to her rape?
        "vupenzi!" ...*juvenile excitement* that led to a lifetime of abuse?
        "vune!" ...*self-inflicted burdens* that keep her up at four?
Trying to outrun her shadows
she's a woman-being, with no soul, like life with no salt
with no beats in her heart, she's a song with no bass—
Woman, like a human no longer being
is her soul scouring for peace
at four in the morning

*kupata – stupid (Karanga)
vupenzi – deranged (Karanga)
vune – deliberate (Karanga)

Travelling by thought

...eyes shut, breath held,
sea-salt crystals diffuse in warm bath swallowing my entirety
all noises mute except my mother's heartbeat
and I savour the snugness of her womb
content and oblivious to my existence
shrinking gradually 'til I float away like a dandelion wish
through a dark tunnel peeling off the veil of ignorance
that has for many seasons enveloped my being
and my knowing returns as I ascend past storeyed realms
'til I reach the seventh dimension at the top of my spine
—a cave opens to nyikadzimu where
Chifedza, Mudzungairi, Chiremba and Nehanda, my spirit guides
usher me through, ululating and jubilating
> *mhondoro dzinomwa munaSave*
> *mhondoro dzinomwa munaSave...*

here, we're fleshless, ageless, sexless, perchance epicene
certainly egoless and selfless, painless
we drink nature's nectar of perennial bliss
speaking not, but conversing through thought
we know truth and I feel my presence here and now
and Mwari's presence is as clear as thought
my memory returns and I begin to recognise
myself in a new light I have not done in the flesh—
I know who I am, and I am home
where suns and moons don't stop illuming their light
all galaxies and their stars beautifully brazen...
residing on the sandy shores of Dziva Guru
a tranquil lake harbouring mermaid spirits
we're backdropped by hills and roaring rivers
and waterfalls with rainbows in nameless hues
grasses and trees perpetually lush with fruit
that can only be picked and savoured by thought...
it is timeless and I don't know how long I've been here or how long I'll stay...
doing only what I love—writing, painting, percussioning
Nhare, Nyunga Nyunga and music instruments I've not seen before

I am mentored by seraphic creatures exuding love ever flowing
like Mwari's omniscience, omnipresence and omnipotence
here, as she is in all dimensions; she is love, I am love and I love it here
'til mhondoro show me woman enduring earthly realm— it is mother(!)
the sacredness of our bond makes me love her at once and that wills my destiny
the cords of which firmly entwine our souls' pledge
      their counsel—*it won't be easy*
      my response—*I can do this*
they usher me back to the cave and I descend my spine via other realms
back to my mother's womb, the darkness of ignorance once again engulfing my being
and when I reach my destination, she pushes me out...
re-entering my flesh back in the water, I am born again—
only to find mother no longer here...

---

*nyikadzimu – a place where our spirit guides / ancestors reside
mhondoro – spirit guide of a particular clan / lions
mhondoro dzinomwa muna Save – lions / spirit guides, drink from the river Save
Dziva Guru – large lake / God
Mwari – the Creator / God
Nhare – a type of mbira / music instrument
Nyunga Nyunga – a type of mbira / music instrument

Blackbird's cry

After The Beatles' *Blackbird*

w
h
e
n
my heart is winter choking on autumn leaves
my head, spring drowning in melting winter ice
my spirit, summer stifled by springtime sprouts
my nerves, autumn seared by summer sunshine,
my voice is blackbird's cry through the seasons
churning. and as times turn, my dead mother
turns up in my dreams to sip
morphine cocktails &

toast
to our
broken
wings
and the
blackbird's
cry is her internal voice,
the cry of the blackbird's chick, her song of songs

In memory of my mother Hilary Fortune M., RIP

Shumirai Nhanhanga

Shumirai Nhanhanga was born in 1965 in Harare (Salisbury then). A teacher by profession, she is also a renowned poet who has managed to break the barrier between male and female Zimbabwean poets. She has written and published short stories and poems under Zimbabwe Women Writers (ZWW) collection of short stories and poetry anthologies, *Light a Candle*, *Totanga Patsva* and *Traps*. She wrote a poetry collection titled *A Shower of Poetic Vistas* which was nominated for the NAMA awards 2016. Shumirai also wrote a drama book titled *Innocent Souls* which was adapted from her short story and published by Progressive Publishers in 2021. Some of her poems have been featured in both print and electronic media.

She has performed at big gatherings such as National Day Commemorations, Zimbabwe International Book Fair and United Nations Programmes. Shumirai has a passion for children, religion and gender issues, and through her performances one is filled with passion and nostalgia. She has sat on various Arts boards such as the Zimbabwe Women Writers, Zimbabwe Association of Theatre for Children and Young People, National Institute of Allied Arts, Zimbabwe Writers' Association, to mention but a few. She has also participated in creating Audio Visual content through Scriptwriting, script editing and audio-visual lesson delivery. Shumirai has helped parents and learners appreciate poetry through her teaching performances.

Siblings

Born of the same mother
But with different characters
Same womb, fed from the same breast
Never the same behaviour
Yet they are still siblings

When something happens in the home
Mother can tell who did it
Even when she was not there
As these are her own babies
These siblings

Surprisingly enough
You disturb one, you disturb them all
Regardless of their own differences
They can solve their own issues
They are siblings

Hello

Hello might be a simple word
But not to the one addressed
As it brings visibility
To the individual being greeted
With a smile there's no need for a reply

Hello might be a way
Of starting a conversation with someone
And when one replies
You know that one is interested to talk
Then the discussion begins

Seeking for someone's attention
When one is in deep thoughts
Without realizing that people are around
And to bring back someone to the scene
Just to say hello

Hello is a form of greeting
To show that you are not alone in a space
But there are others or someone within
Remember to always respond when one says HELLO

Talent

Picked at a tender age
During early childhood learning
Managing to stand in front of others
Saying out news and stories without being manipulated
Displaying a talent

Singing music, bringing out melody
Music that soothes the mind
And when the singer or musician does this
Bringing joy to the people
Or sending listeners and viewers
Down memory lane
That's a talent

Never be shy to showcase your talent
For you never know whom you inspire
Or whom you are training and uplifting
Through performances or displays
Avoid putting your talent in the closet
For it is your talent

Sibonginkosi Christabel Netha

Sibonginkosi is a poet from the city of Bulawayo, Zimbabwe. Under the stage name "Siboe" she has been performing poetry since 2017 and writing poetry for as long as she can remember. In 2019 she was a finalist in the Lafarge Poetry Slam and in 2021 she was a finalist in the Time of the Writer Poetry. Her selected pieces were published in the Poetry for Human Rights Publication.

In 2018 she was a finalist in the Africa Book Club short story competition for her entry, 'The Baby's Mother'. She also contributed three short stories to *Turquoise Dreams* – an anthology by Zimbabwean women.

As a young woman who has lived in Chipinge and Bulawayo (Zimbabwe) and Johannesburg (South Africa), the concept of home and belonging inspires a lot of her work. Sibonginkosi is passionate about social development, so when she's not writing or performing, she can be found working with young people in the non-profit sector.

A Meaningless Story

I sweep the leaves away from the door.
The wind blows them back immediately.
I sweep the jacaranda blossom in the yard today.
Tomorrow morning the ground is covered in purple again.
We declare our undying love for each other now.
Tomorrow I find you in the arms of another.
When will I realize
the futility of it all?

There was a Void
After Warsan Shire

There was always something missing.
It wasn't just the money.
We packed up three whole childhoods
in a single backpack and left,
jumped over the border and let
the wind take us away.
We drifted far
until only faded memories remained.

Growing up I had no photos of myself.
I did not even know
which day of the week I was born.
It was not supposed to matter.
We were fed and getting an education.
Why should we care
that we felt sad and alienated?
Growing up we were not supposed to speak
in the dialect of back home.
It's "imoto" not "mota",
each syllable a tool for protection,
your tone a step towards survival.
Do not speak too loud or you'll put us in danger.
Do not dare mention the word Zimbabwe.
Make friends but do not let them get too close...

Growing up we never knew what to do with emotions.
We suppressed and stifled anything that felt real.
We sought perfection and only ever wanted the good.
We blocked out the trauma, gave ourselves new personas,
rewrote our storylines and pretended the shark could not get us
because if home was the mouth of the shark then we were safe.
Because whatever had once resembled home to our souls
was now a gaping hole much greater than Kimberley,
an unending void, echoing our need for belonging.

Bird of Paradise

Feathers of vibrant hues
singing a golden tune
you
are not of this world.
You have always been something of an oddity
something to marvel at.
Your presence is borderline culture shock
to those who think only in black and white.
You sing tunes that befuddle
those who listen in straight lines
you are the C minor of a jazz tune
here to bewilder and amaze.
You are the melancholy of a saxophone solo
pulling at the misery in our hearts
giving it a home to live in your music.

Oh bird of paradise!
You are unfamiliar territory
the road not taken
you are the difference between home and away
the no man's land between who we are
and what we aspire to be.
Knowing you is like a trip into the jungle
leaving behind everything we know
just to behold the beauty you are
and to experience the awe and wonder.
There's so much power
where you are.

Oh! bird of paradise!
You sing songs that fill my heart with sadness
and joy
all at the same time!
You make me ponder difficult questions –
Like how on earth did a beauty like you

come to live in the same earth as a grey thing like me?
Like how on earth did you find yourself in a dry land like this?
Like how on earth can you still sing beautiful songs
when there is no beauty left to see?

Oh! bird of paradise!
Feathers of vibrant hues
singing a golden tune
you
are not of this world.

Twin Lollipops

Twin lollipops
leave wagging tongues,
to be waved this way and that
by juvenile hands
As the school day is reviewed:
"Who took whose pen and never gave it back?"
Jokes are retold
and laughter flows from soft bellies.
Two juvenile hearts
beating under hot khaki shirts
experience a connection.
Twin lollipops re-enter
the contented mouths of youngsters
to leave a dewy sweetness
 rivalled only by the sweet taste of friendship.

Siphathisiwe Mitchel Lunga

Siphathisiwe Mitchel Lunga is a law student at Midlands State University. She has participated in various national and regional moot court competitions, in which she has done very well. Raised in Lower Gwelo by parents who are both teachers, she grew up immersed in literature. She is a Zimbabwean blogger on http://www.tug-it.blogspot.com whose writings are inspired by societal issues, especially those affecting women and young people in Zimbabwe. Her writings on http://www.chroniclesofalawintern.blogspot.com are a chronicle of her life and experiences as a Zimbabwean law student.

Mother Nation

They said a nation is a mother,
They said that her love is fierce, she is a lioness.
Jealously, she protects her offspring.
They said a nation is a mother.

They said no harm shall befall her children,
Mother Nation is a champion.
She destroys adversaries with a justified vengeance.
They said a nation is a mother.

They forgot to say, my Mother is a monster,
Her fangs and claws gouge her children's souls.
She thirsts after the blood of her offspring.
They said a nation is a mother.

My Mother dances to the sound of her children's cries.
As if to a lullaby, she sleeps to their wailings.
She loves the sounds of their cries, their tears are art.
They said a nation is a mother.

Of leg chains and prisons for her children, she dreams.
Her soul drips of venom.
She merries at the perish of their dreams,
Smiles at the extinction of her offspring.
They said a nation is a mother.
My Mother is a Monster.

On Prayers

Prayers_
A pocketful from my father,
Bags of them from my mother.
Some uttered at the altar of thanksgiving,
Body, soul and mind as surrender.
Some uttered in islands of tears,
Hoping to resuscitate dreams from ashes,
Like Lazarus from dust.

Prayers_
A pocketful answered,
Bags of them unheard.
Wishes left in the hands of cosmic forces,
Did we ever need constellations to hang our dreams on?
Did we need to let our words uttered in confidence travel past galaxies
That suffocated them before they could reach higher ears?

Scents and Stars

The scent of unfulfilled dreams lingers.
It is present in every inhale as the aroma of burnt meat
is present in each bite.
Born into sorrow, we learnt to dance under the weeping sky,
hoping that under nights like these, stars will be birthed
and chapters of light conceived.
Yet here we are,
still clutching the hems of a night so dark it knows no moon.
Exhaling the scent of broken dreams is only accepting the truth
that bears the loss of light.

Foreign Accents

What can we talk about—
We whose voices have recorded no discovery,
We whose ancestors adopted a foreign identity?

What can we talk about—
We whose tongues are twisted in the clutches of a foreign tongue,
We who do not remember to laugh in our mother tongue?

What can we talk about—
We whose fantasies are made of doses of Westerners,
We who are not strong enough to handle our blackness?

The Poem

It was recorded not on paper;
Neither did it go on a date with ink.
It was reflected not in her eyes;
Nor did the mouth whisper it.

The real poetry was carved across decades of inner turmoil.
Its beat: the screams the world chanted.
Its form and zenith:
The constant need to prove the world wrong.

The poem was engraved on the blisters on her hands.
Its metaphors, massacres at home.
Its bubbles, a battle against life's giants.

The real poetry was written in streams of tears;
Lashings from chains and whips long enough to reach her heart.
The real poetry was one she never talked of.
Neither did she write it down on paper.

Miracles

Burning filaments cover patches of torn hope
Turbulent torrents, shadows of splintered dreams.
Yet with hands cut short and feet strapped to concrete
She still jumps at fireflies,
Hoping to freeze their sparkle in her heart.
But gravity is undefeated.

A face mangled beyond layers of cracking powder.
Cheap scent, a smell of despair mingling in vain embrace.
Gorged and deflated,
Her being shatters as her mirror breaks
In shards, a pattern of scattered hope around her fragility.
Glass breaks too.

Sue Nyakubaya-Nhevera

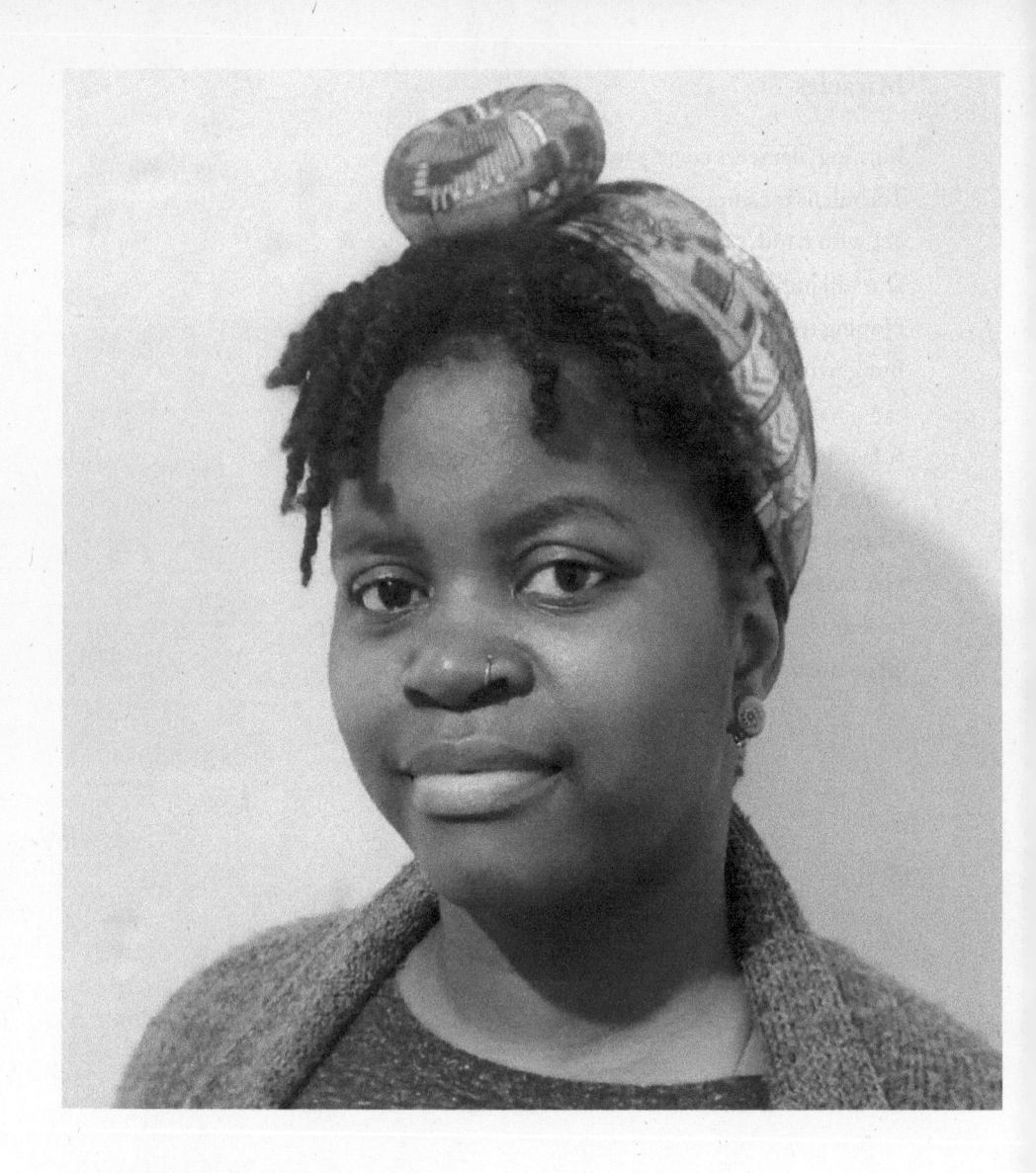

Sue Nyakubaya-Nhevera is an award-winning blogger, winning The Fresh Voice Afrobloggers Award in 2020. Born and raised in Harare, she started writing poetry in her late teens. She finds inspiration in everything around her. Her works have been published on various platforms and mediums including *Zimbolicious:Poetry Anthology Volume 2* and *Zimbolicious: An Anthology of Zimbabwean Literature and Arts Volume 3* by Mwanaka Media and Publishing, as well as a self-published chapbook, *The Rivers We Cry: A Chapbook,* in addition to features on various online platforms. She is passionate about literature and equality. Sue currently lives in South Africa with her husband and toddler. You can find more of her works on her blog, Amari Online Blog.

Fragrances

Hold my hand
Take me to the time I can't remember
So I can lace together
Memories forgotten
Bring pictures to life
With fragrances that draw me back
To childhood memories
To laughter and carefree souls
To a mind that dreamt of the impossible
And if you can
Let time stand still
So I can picture the now
Envision the future me
Indulge in memories gone

Failing Feet

They never said it would be easy
I never expected it to be
But every time
Those feet fail you
My heart can't help but dissolve
Into tears you may never see fall
Ones I will forever feel
Scars form in places
You will never know exist
Hard exteriors are made
But the softness within
Will never be touched
When those feet start failing you
Try to find balance, please
Spare my heart

Time-travel

Grandpa clock
Whisk me
To the future
Give me a glimpse
Of the me to come
She may drop a pearl of wisdom
Or two
Give me some sound advice
Tell me the fro
Will grow in due time
That I can fix
My crown on my own
But it's OK
To ask for help if need be
She will tell me to be patient
And remember not to break myself
As I bend over backwards for others
That being invisible
Or trying my darndest to be is fine
But if I trip
I must recall
That I have a trampoline
Of people
Ready to bounce me back to solid ground

Childhood Feels Like Home

Childhood looks like dust-covered feet at sunset
Making their way through the broken fence
After my mother's call for supper

Childhood smells like blood dripping from big toe
You know the one that collided with this tarmac road
During a game of hwishu

Childhood tastes like sadza mbodza rembida
Made in hole-riddled pots salvaged from the rubbish hill next to the road
It tastes like the freedom of our carefree ways

Childhood sounds like laughter when we joke at others' expense
It sounds like sobs over broken friendships
That we know will be mended by sunrise tomorrow

Childhood feels like the warmth of soup on an extra chilly day
It feels like hugs from friends long gone, friends never to be seen again
Childhood feels like home, it's why we never grow old but stay young at heart

*Hwishu is a children's game.
 Sadza mbodza rembida is a type of undercooked thick porridge.

Wind

Gust of wind
Take me with you
Teach me
Your carefree ways

How you pick up
All that's willing
To be taken
And become yours

How to leave
What's too heavy
That which is too much of a burden
That, not deserving of your strength

Teach me how
To be silent yet speak volumes
To yield when I should
To unleash wrath when I must

Gust of wind
Most of all
Teach me
Gentleness

Tariro Ndoro

Tariro's debut poetry collection, *Agringada: Like a Gringa, Like a Foreigner*, was the recipient of the NAMA Award for an Outstanding Poetry Book in 2020 and she has also been shortlisted for the DALRO Poetry Prize, the BN Poetry Prize and the Intwasa Short Story Competition. Her poetry, fiction and essays have been published in numerous international literary journals. Tariro was a Spring '22 International Writing Programme Fellow.

Hunting

Observe...

 A good man shoots an eland once:
 Between the eyes
 Kill shot
     and
 It falls.

 When a narco kills a boar
 He hurts it in the flank and
 Tracks it by its life-blood
 The pheromone of fear
 Almost edible on his tongue
 Sweet
 Addictive
 This too is a metaphor

  You may play roulette with a trophy hunter
  But know this:
  He'll load six bullets to the chamber
  Nothing's left to chance

Bodies

it was the summer of coffins and dying
that is to say, there were posters out for uyinene
or maybe just before that...

and I remember, she should never have died alone & nobody should ever die alone
and she must not have gone gentle into the good night because who goes peacefully when they're staring down a barrel of a gun

    and it's a cruel thing to leave a body unburied and alone and exposed and shameful so much more that a good Samaritan pointed her stolen car to a member of the SAPS, and he refused to stop and search because there was no probable cause and there was no justification or jurisdiction but still a woman is dead that could've been alive and no one cared (enough)

    and it was just yesterday she was alive and in one of my classes and I never said goodbye to her because she would live to get old and fat and wrinkled (or so I thought)

    and in that spring too there was uyinene and we must remember he had more skeletons in his backyard and those girl's names were never mentioned on the eight o'clock news and too there is my friend, who remembers the shock of bearing audio witness to a murder/suicide:

- one scrape of a chair against a wooden floor
- three raised voices in the middle of the night
- two gun shots and
- silence

    and he must have thought it was another columbine or something because he sat there and waited for death to find him and it never came, but the yellow tape on the next door told him he hadn't misheard a single thing: this is what happens when a woman tries to leave and a man decides he ~~cannot~~ will not live without her so

  he
  takes
  his
  own
  life
        but

    is too big a coward to face the afterlife alone, he takes women and children with
him and there is no one left behind to continue the family line that
is the way
    of things

and there is the room-mate:
—*what do you do when you hear domestic violence?*
—when did it happen?
—*now like five minutes ago*
—you mean to say it's happening now?

and each time it feels asynchronous:
the sun shines
& someone plays music
& a life is lost
&
they all have names:
amanda uyinene meghan roommate

those who know death know this too—
it is the true sign of grief to transcend weeping
those who have lost know how an empty heart beats,
heavily

Thandokuhle Cleo Sibanda

Thandokuhle is a spoken word artist whose poetry is primarily driven by expression and inspired by anything and everything that triggers thought and emotion. She began her journey over five years ago when she was still in high school, inspired and ushered by her Accounts teacher and renowned poet Sithandazile Dube. Her first stage appearance was at a competition commemorating Bulawayo at 100 years and she came out second. In the same year she entered Intwasa Arts Festival competitions where she also scooped some prizes. She proceeded to be a multiple slam champion, Starbrite finalist and award nominee. She has performed in some of the biggest stages locally, such as the Shoko Arts Festival in Harare, Intwasa Arts Festival, Bulawayo Arts Awards and some internationally, such as the SADC Human Rights and Poetry Festival, Poets in Joburg. She has been a curtain raiser for the likes of Joseph Solomon, and shared stages with renowned artists such as Tariro neGitare, Edith Wewutonga, Nkwali, Thandi Dhlana, Batsirai Chigama, Tinashe Tafirenyika, Holy Ten, Siphokazi Jonas, amongst many others. She has also worked with organisations such as UNESCO, Japanese embassy and Moto Republik under the ResiliArt Accelerator Program, Alpha Media Holdings, YETT, Citizen's Manifesto, and WILD.

Maybe, Maybe Not

I'm not quite the ancestors' dream but I could stand in for a few cousins if they fell under the weather or got stuck in traffic or something

I'm not the brightest student, nor the loudest but if you visit the class often enough I think you'll notice me

I'm not exactly average but I'm not outstanding either

I've been second best in a lot of things so I guess that counts for something right

I'm not an alpha, but I'm not like the rest of the pack either

I'm like the other E-d from Ed, Edd n Eddy

I don't think I'm mediocre

But I'm not exactly genius or anything close to perfect or willing to go the extra mile

I'm more standard, but I do extra things once in a while

I'm an introvert but within context

I'm smart but often silent during debates because I don't like speaking at the top of my voice

And Poetry...
It's the one thing I'm both amazing and terrible at

A Lot Like Barbie

Raised by an army of icons that looked a lot like things out of reach
Things that can only be dreamt about
Things that normally get stuck in wild imaginings and places where only fantasies could take us
A lot like unicorns
Flying pigs
Maybe looking like cookie cut-out versions of a plastic doll crafted by human beings raised with a singular standard of what looks pretty...
A lot like Barbie

Being humble chested in a world that calls for breasts to pose as shields and fists battling against faces that don't look flawless, things not in the right places,
To compensate for what's not conventionally all right
Being humble chested surrounded by people who base first impressions on how well boobies say hi
On how well they protrude and just how long they can sustain a conversation
Perfectly round and just the right size
A lot like...Barbie

A world that names all kinds of breasts, some with an undertone of shaming
East West?
They are side by side but they don't have to head towards the same direction
Widely set?
Some chests are heavier and could use the space in between
Narrow?!
Description says "breasts are thin and nipples are pointing down"
Maybe the sadness in our hearts finds shelter in our breasts and wears them down.
The good ones get names like
Round
Teardrop
Bell shape
Oranges
Apples
A whole lot like Barbie

My Therapist Says

Border line set between borders,

A few sins from falling over to the other side but just the same amount of prayers to be saved

A few *I can't do this anymore's* from throwing in the towel but also a few more strides forward to the breaks you've been striving for

You're a ball of fire but you're moving in reverse, you're both hot and cold, you're here, you're there all at the same time

I can see you're breathing but when I look deeper into your eyes I see void

Like your soul packed up to leave sometime ago and never looked back

You're a shapeshifter, your identities come at you all at once

Your tears are both suicide notes and a tribute to life,

expressions of gratitude and requests for more out of it

It's never a good day or a bad one

Maybe your brain is floating, your whole being defies gravity and everything that grounds us

Your world is completely different from ours

I can't scale you

I can't solve you

You're neither here nor there,

You're everywhere all at once

The Streets That Raise Us

Waking up to the sound of hoots and chants from young men proposing wheels that take you to the centre of chaos at a price different from one they asked for yesterday,
Best believe it won't be the same when it's time for them to bring you back to your place of rest
It's not coffee that you'll smell when your nostrils take the first sniff,
It's the dust from women all across the block dressing yards, because on this side of town
We don't own tars or pavements that conceal our poverty
You stretch out your arm to wake your cousin to wake your cousin next to her,
Unlike you, their ears are still blocked by hopes and dreams sold in tenth grade,
Their eyes haven't seen what you have seen so they don't fight to stay open,
Their shoulders are yet to feel the load of expectation and failure so they know just how to lie back and relax,
Unlike you, their inner selves haven't yet waged war against them
  So, hoots and chants metres away are no
  match for their very sound sleep

Waking up already exhausted and worn out by the day
But you're too broke to stay home watching your peers and old men alike lose their lives to the bottle and girls your age aging way faster than you
You still have a few bars of ambition left so that'll take you through the day
A day of misery and make believe
It's easy to make what you're doing sound important around here, all you have to say is "I work for an NGO"
But what you forget to mention is you're practically doing the Lord's work
Your work depends on small handouts from bigger fish and you haven't had those in a while so you might not make rent next month let alone get a pay check

But you're trying really
Putting your best foot forward and all.
Climbing out of this side of town isn't exactly easy,
There's too much weight pulling you down
Your accent, crustiness
The schools you went to,
The pockets just haven't been deep enough

Before all these other things that set you up for a good one,
You need to eat and feed your cousins
It's not just you you're trying to save,
It's a whole generation...

It Won't Count

Lands that have grown dry and eventually barren continue to harbour drought for as long as they are left unploughed

They will continue to call out the names of carts and bulls that once ploughed it to plug in roots of harvest,

Their tears will never make it to the surface and they will continue to be the earth that houses the dry bones of our ancestors

Who also died calling out titles of the supposed fathers and heroes but were never named or shamed,

The crimes that drove out their souls using poverty and injustice as tools,

were never brought to light or tried

Because none of them

Spoke about a home they want beyond bonfires, kombis and bhawas

None of them ever took it upon themselves to put the cross upon themselves and drag it home to freedom

All of them had something to say about what wasn't right but none was brave enough to do something about it

* bhawas – bar

Tsitsi Ella Jaji

Tsitsi's most recent volume of poetry, *Mother Tongues* (2019) received the Cave Canem Northwestern University Press Prize. Her first collection, *Beating the Graves* (2017), and a chapbook, *Carnaval* (2014), were published by the African Poetry Book Fund. Jaji was born and raised in Zimbabwe, and moved to the U.S. to study piano and literature. Her poems often evoke music, the sacred, migrancy, and ecological crisis.

Jaji is the Mary S. Bevington Associate Professor of Modern Poetry in English and African & African American Studies at Duke University, and has been fortunate to have held fellowships at the Mellon New Directions, National Humanities Center, and Radcliffe Institute for Advanced Studies. She is the author of *Africa in Stereo: Music, Modernism and Pan-African Solidarity*, which received the African Literature Associations First Book award, and honourable mentions for the Kwabena Nketia Award (Society for Ethnomusicology) and Harry Levin Prize (American Comparative Literature Association).

The Spread

It's dark here, when my daughter smileys me
"Good morning, kkkkkk." We fill our morning's
eyes with each other. An apology's parenthesis
is bested – Uncle Love, his actual name, tells me
about the architectural plans for a kitchen in Detroit
and the radio station. We drink Tanganda instead
of coffee.

          Half my mind is reading the WhatsApps
from my other daughter, off to court for brewing
beer under the table.
                        My other mind will text
a caveat to her elder sister – my father may be too far gone
to know exactly who she is, maybe not the best one
to give the ancestral nod to a divorce council.
Still, I promise to ask. My personal opinion, I thumb on,
is that mukwasha is a drunk and she should leave him,
and let the rent come due.

                    My small boy's protests will interrupt us.
December 6's advent chocolate masks the flag of Wales.
Today, Gabriel picks a name for Joseph.
I tell him these are stories, and hope that's all there is to it.

Charmed, last night I let him play gudo to my tsuro, live action.
Later I will walk through a tiered garden from the office
back to my car. I will notice the kale here is an ornament
and think to myself, "Isn't that rich."

---

* Mukwasha – son-in-law
  Gudo and Tsuro – baboon and hare; characters in a beloved Shona tale

moving mom to my brother's: an alzheimer's poem

my touch no lighter than
theirs, I see that letting go
must begin, anew.

when donepezil
is discontinued, the mind
may blur, or else, stir.

michelle doctors our soul.
her counsel: time to let
disease take its course.

i thought my rage, my
tiger daughter meetings, my
tenderness would stop

wanderings and starts:
a peeping tom, a shadow,
phantom staff stealing her slacks.

They will keep her safe.
They will love her husband,
he is their father too, of course.

Wadzanai Tadhuvana

"There is no greater agony than bearing an untold story inside you", Maya Angelou wrote in *I know why the caged bird sings*. These words speak to Wadzanai and spur her to keep writing. Wadzanai, also known as "Wadzie Tads", is an award-winning writer who writes to deal with life, the joys and pains that she sees, her thoughts and feelings, and most importantly to express herself. Writing is her breath; she must write to live. She has a full-time job as a Chartered Accountant, which she loves. However, to borrow from the words of Anton Chekov: Accounting is lawful wife and literature the mistress!

Not Loved, Not Held

I, John Chimutashu, take you, Wadzanai, to be my wife.

I promise to love you as you are, not as I want you to be.
But daily I am reminded that even a baby hippo has got nothing on me.
I lost the plot when I gave birth.

I promise to laugh, hug and cuddle, no matter what life throws at us.
Work.
Boys' nights out.
Hustling.
Oh, the lonely nights I have spent by myself.

I long to grow old with you and share all that I have with you.
They are your finances, John,
You constantly remind me of that!
The properties are in your name!

I promise to love you always,
To be faithful to you, to listen to you,
And to never take you for granted.
John, your sisters always tell me to persevere.
That is how marriage is like,
To stay for the children.
Inherently, monogamy is a western concept, they tell me.

I promise to protect you when you are vulnerable,
To admire you when you are strong.
"The problem is that you want to be a man," you always tell me,
"I am the father of this house, the head of this family."

I promise to challenge you to be the best version of yourself,
To support your dreams, no matter how wild they are.
Oh well, they have remained just that, wild dreams!

Dreams

I dream of a day when getting home after work will not be a hassle.

I will simply finish my work, walk to the bus station, get into a bus and arrive home with my dignity intact.

The transport is never enough.

Thus, when it comes, there is pressure,

Pressure to get into the transport.

And some take the opportunity to release their pressure.

Long queues characterise my commute home.

Pickpockets feast on me as I wait!

Some try to molest me. Some succeed.

My dignity is always stripped on my way home.

Either I sit at the back at the mercy of the weather,

Or I stand the whole way.

But either way, I must pick up my dignity when I alight so that I get home with it intact.

I long for a day where I will use safe and dignified transport.

I will have a seat.

My luggage will be safe.

The speed will be legal and safe.

I can voice my concerns and I will have recourse.

I will not be molested

Or robbed.

I will pay a fair price that is in sync with what I earn.

My dignity will be with me always!

I will be safe.

The Burden of Culture

When they come into your house
You greet them with a smile on your face,
Even when it is raining in your heart
And your thoughts are so far away in the distance.
Even when you know that their presence will kill a part of you,
You must be strong,
You have visitors.
Fake it till you make it!
Put that smile on your face!
Your parents raised you to be pleasant.

For the visitors will give a report of their treatment,
Shaping perceptions about you for a lifetime.

You greet them because they are older than you.
They are your elders,
Even when they do not act in a manner befitting of elders.
Fake it till you make it!
Put that smile on your face!
Who knows, you could be ministering to angels?

When makoti takes abuse, threats and violence from "mother in love"
She puts a smile on her face.
For without "mother in love",
Makoti would not have her husband.

When "mother in love" is snubbed,
Neglected, with accusations of witchcraft directed her way,
She puts a smile on her face.
For makoti is now her son's number one
And she has been relegated to second division.

It is hardest to be oneself with family.
There are norms and expectations that must be fulfilled
While perceptions are developed.
It is the burden of culture.

*Makoti – daughter-in-law.

Zahirra Dayal

Zahirra was made in Zimbabwe and has lived in four different countries. London is currently her home. She fell in love with the sound, taste and colour of words the moment she was old enough to ride her red bicycle to the Harare City Library in Rotten Row. In her writing she likes to explore and interrogate the unspoken and the uncomfortable. Her debut novel in progress won the Jericho Writers' Friday Night Live and has been listed for prizes including Mslexia, Owned Voices, The Deborah Rogers Writing Award, The Laura Kinsella Fellowship and The SI Leeds Literary Prize. Her short stories have been published in various literary magazines including The Mechanics Institute Review. You can read her stories at www.zahirradayal.com.

De-frizz, De-melanate, Diminish

Tame those curls,
iron that frizz,
relax the bush,
scorch it into submission.
Hide from the sun,
brighten it,
whiten it,
de-melanate.
Nod and smile,
say yes,
cross your legs,
until your wedding night.
Clamp your mouth,
temper your wild laugh,
scooch to the edge.
Crouch,
bend,
contort your bigness.
Cover your curves,
sit still,
prettify.
The roof's the limit.
Tomboys and
troublemakers
unwanted here.

Ubiquitous Fear

It lives in my stomach
where it free floats with no anchor
it rises and falls
with my shallow breaths
it screams from every pore
it's alive on the hairs of my skin
in the whites of my eyes
and the pink of my lips
it pulses through the bluey purple veins
under the surface of my skin
it whispers from the spaces
between my words
it resides in my footfalls
it lurks in the shadows of my shadow
haunting my breath
pounding my head
choking my voice.

The Yellow House

Off the main road
in a leafy cul-de-sac
is a yellow house
where the trees in the back garden
are heavy with overripe things
and the front veranda
is crowded with garden chairs painted in rust
inside the yellow house
in the leafy cul-de-sac
pot plants come to die
and monsters hide in the light
of familial immunity
debauchery lives under sparkling white robes
insecurity resides in puffed up chests and
hands that strike and choke
anger inhabits clenched white teeth
and shame crawls beneath grease-soaked rugs
liquid guilt fills half-moon bags
under dulled black eyes
in the yellow house
off the main road
in the leafy cul-de-sac
pain is a second skin
and a miasma of fear coats everything
animosity lies behind veneers of civility
and self-hatred ducks under finger-stained mirrors
in the yellow house
off the main road
in a leafy cul-de-sac

Autumn

The musky-sweet tang of autumn
serrates the air.
A heady mix of decay,
transition and rebirth.
Leaves rust and curl,
twisting free of maternal boughs.
Like copper diamonds
they dance
and caress the light
playing with the wind,
and then they fall asleep.
Mother Nature
knows to rest
before the slap of winter.

Where are you really from?

my ancestors' umbilical cords
are buried here, there, everywhere
But where are you really from?
I'm here now
But your hair?
It doesn't matter
But your skin?
It doesn't matter
But your accent?
It's all the places my feet have been

I'd rather be an outsider
and dance in the margins
than
be fixed to a centre that doesn't adapt or bend,

I'd rather be immersed in kaleidoscopic multiplicity
than
be painted with a single hue,
I'd rather gaze at the world from different vantage points
than
cling to my singular worldview.

I'd rather luxuriate in the wide-open spaces
of never fitting in
than
squeeze myself into baskets with immovable labels.

What do you mean racist?

It's in your condescending grin
and the angle of your brows
when you frown at me
from across the room.
It's in the way you turn around
to check your purse
when I'm behind you
at the traffic lights.
It's in the way
you pretend
to pack the shelves
to keep an eye
while I browse.
It's in the way
you hand me my towel
and single me out
to check my gym card.
It's in the way your eyes land on me
when I enter your space
and the way your smile
doesn't stretch across your face.
It's in the way my presence irks you
and the way you despise me
before I've opened my mouth.
It's a seed planted and nurtured in you
over generations.
It's nothing I can pinpoint or articulate
I only know the churning in my gut and bones

Zaza Muchemwa

Zaza (poet, short story writer, dramatic arts practitioner) authored the short story, 'Dance with yesterday' and the play, *The IVth Interrogation*. Her poetry has been published on Pen International website, Badilisha Poetry Xchange, in Zimbabwean Newspapers and included in the Zimbabwe Poets for Human Rights Anthology, *All Protocols Observed* and Cyphers Poetry Anthology Volume 87. She has written for Index on Censorship Magazine, Povo Magazine, MUD Journal and other publications. Zaza is an award-winning theatre director and producer, directing several productions including *The Incident* by Joakim Daun which won the 2018 NAMA Award for outstanding theatre production, and *How are you really?* by Chiedza Rwodzi, which won a NAMA award for outstanding theatrical production and Zaza a NAMA award for outstanding director for 2022.

Zaza is the Associate Artistic Director for Almasi Collaborative Arts, and the Chairperson of the Zimbabwe Centre of International Theatre Institute. Recently, Zaza took part in the International Writing Program Fall Residency 2022 at the University of Iowa.

She

She is a storyteller with no ink
to tell the stories that are sealed
behind walls too paper thin
that have kept the thread from reaching the end.
She is a raving wind
blowing the mind into tiny pieces
that fall upon ears cotton wooled
that listen to rhymes and can't hear the reason
we can't dance to reason
we can't move to reason
we can't listen to reason.
To the rhymes they make a mecca
the blood that flows in her veins
is a cocktail of styles
she, the storyteller, has made up in her mind
rhymes she has felt
as she has walked along walls
that have kept their stories
only to tell her
with no ink
cannot write with glee
her graffiti upon   his story
to make her story come true,
She   is a storyteller with no ink
Let her live
Let her speak.

Under Your Spell

Crushed flowers lining the pathway
A way to your heart
Bleeding they wilt to death
Quashed by the disdain of your regard
      Love, you have killed me.

Bite my lips to stay the pain
Fold my tongue to imprison your name
Underneath the words I am going to say
So I will not say it,
That I have stitched my undergarments with thoughts of you
And when I prick myself
I will bleed your name.

Fervently waiting for the sun to shine
In my overzealousness punch holes in my heart
When I try to erase the memory of your face
I find myself looking at you
Every pore of myself leaking,
      breaking in sweat.

Come to this midnight party
The sacrifice?
My head on a platter
And no don't treat it like it's chicken shit
This is my brain.

Snail's freedom
Its pace disregarding the passage of time
Under the cocoon of warm blankets
Dig the hole deeper

Where I bury my dreams of you
Hiding the images
Shielding the pictures from the reality of daylight.

Overflowing with masses for freedom
Each ritual lasting no more than a minute
Erect an epitaph on my pillow
To remind me of your absence
Reminding myself of your presence
In my body, my brain, my thoughts
My system malfunctioning, malfunctioned by a mantra
You, you, you, you and more you.

Escape on a sigh,
      a wish
Try hard as I might
My defences are too weak to fight this
So, I ride on the wave of this,
A freeway to hell
Watching the carnage helplessly my heart endures
Hoping that I do have a return ticket.

Crushed flowers
Lining the pathway
A way to your heart
Bleeding they wilt to death
Dashed by the scorn of your gaze
      Love, you have killed me

'Not another political poem'

This is not a political poem,
 I SAID,
'This is not a political poem,'
It is not another political poem.
But have you heard?
That:
Your children are
being fashioned out of hollow fruit
Your sons have been
turned into murderers
of the moon,
blood red is the colour
borrowed from the toil of their hands.
Your daughters have been abandoned by their own shadows,
there is no daylight nor moonlight in the countries they have been
bundled into.
Your children are making
trends out of empty harvests
yet they remain unseen, unheard; their tales unspoken.
Fear and dread know them by their number.
Strife jests with their bones before the spirit is wrested from flesh
Not another political poem, is it?

Psalms from Concrete

Cement floors hold on tightly to marked spaces
Bones floating reach skin boundaries
Flowing in undulating waves,
Plaintive cries
Babies cooing
Moans crescendoing
On matchsticks
On combustible elements – open flames
Sometimes red-hot electric plates,
Hunger reaches
It shoots up
And boils down.
Desire sparks like unwired energy shots
As distressed hope finds a cure in imagination's figments
The earth's firmaments shake through
Blood congealed; blood un-congealed
Unconditional is the race beyond crumbling walls
A hallelujah, an amen
Perhaps a yes to million questions bouncing in space unasked
Cement floors fade, making way for tarmac spaces
Bones find their place, carrying hearts
Heart still yearning for possession of the concealed packets of freedom
Red hot fire burns the mind
Red liquid pumps within delineated spaces of skin and bones
Keeping peace between warring states is the secret delicately nestled
In a life source buried somewhere in concrete.

Manifesto

when lights go off
we scurry
we have been told darkness is our enemy
it envelops body, captures souls in cocoons of emptiness,
we, the multitudes, live on two breads alone...
      'bury myself before they kill me. dig my own shallow grave before I
          am disappeared in crocodile pits...'
of the internet shutdown we bear in the barrenness of our dying fields
our protest voices gurgling on rusty irons...
         'kill you with tetanus first.'
we live in illegal times:
masticated ulcerated rhymes commit crimes against our universe.
life has become an illegal, cloaking itself in auras of madness,
freedom fighters gripped by cruel masters of greed
destroying our leaders for more gold and platinum...
life has become an illicit, stuffing her voice on platitudes
of angry little men riding on stilts of gun ambition...
she, the oracle, was going to pave a way for all of us,
in fear of her haunting ghost
angry little men may build a statue in her name...
        'next time tumirai mago, nyuchi dzinokurigwa.'
order! order! order?
we don't need that kind of order
not squares, not rectangles, no triangles please, just circular
in the name of humanity's safe passage to the next timeline
we refuse treaties of forceful order,
we refuse trade-offs which suffocate, maim, and kill...
disappear off earth's face traces of human races,
humans are living under the Act of No Mercy
with fear enterprise misguiding them and stepping on the airways of their dreams
today darkness smites light
soon we shall learn to embrace it
we will befriend darkness till we are one
in it we birth ourselves anew

we need new faces, new voices, new names for the bodies on the street...
we, the multitudes, are springing forth in our power
we rise from certain death to new life orders
we revolt from extinction to remould lights
which burn bright enough to eclipse the dimness of want
to reshape the shades of misrule
for our own unfettering.

* 'next time tumirai mago, nyuchi dzinokurigwa.' – 'next time send wasps, bees will be defeated.' (Karanga

Rain Dance

i come with the rain
plunging deep into pockets of rain
i make the air sing
so, there is no pain
when the valleys ring
with the names etched on stone walls of ancient kingdoms
i ease the blood flowing in
voices dancing in the concrete pathways of succeeding queendoms
making pots fill the soil with
the suns and moons of millennia
strung in the beaded sweat of the peasant
hoeing the future from the past
hovering in the background
       are:
feet tapping
hands clapping
freedom untying from circular pots holding ancient wisdom
these are
       words that have told this land to stay
       when the drain of life would have made it die
me and my people – we have sung songs
gone to caves of mountains
where we have planted the seed for the harvest
       babies crying in delight
   tomorrow they will have their bellies full
we come with the rain
washing over our ebony bodies
air and substance follow us today
tomorrow is a plan being put to work
so put the gourd of beer in the middle of the circle
our parched throats are ready.

Zenith Bvukutwa

Zenith was born and raised in Zimbabwe. She studied her Bachelor's degree in Applied Arts at the University of Zimbabwe and got an Honours in French. She also holds a Master's degree in Cultural Innovation from University of Transilvania, Brasov in Romania where she currently resides. She can speak Shona, English and Romanian. Zenith is also a professional signed model. Besides reading and writing, Zenith enjoys dancing, karaoke and hanging out with friends in the sun. Zenith can be reached at zenithbvukutwa@gmail.com.

A Coffee and a Cigarette

Funny how coffee brings out the differences in people.

For some it's a way of life, a guilty pleasure,

For my sister it's a test of her faith and patience.

She looks at me, her assailant, like I'm shitting in front of her

For besmirching the holy ground that is her home, with the smell of coffee.

Judgement is written on her face,

But she won't give in to the devil and open her mouth.

Her frown alone does the job, and I can feel the hot charcoal from heaven showering my soul.

I hide the cigarette.

If she smells it,

God and his angels would not be able to shield me from the wrath that will descend upon me.

Wish List

In the next life
If God has woken up
I want to come back as I am

With shapely legs that beckon men
Raging confidence for slapping wandering hands
Without the sad eyes that have accepted the fate of the world

My parents would be richer
My mother would choose a better husband
There would be no racism
Kidding, of course
Africa would colonise Europe
And rob Asia and America of their humanity

Again

Shhhh....Focus, she chided herself
First relationship after THE BREAKUP
Always a transition, nerves, anxiety all crippling her to her fingertips
Her eyes downcast, ready to look away.
She willed herself to focus on the naked man.

His hands trembled, feverishly
He paused, hands on her swollen behind
Like his predecessor, he lingered, fondling.

She tilted her head upwards, opening space for his mouth
His hands rougher than she was used to, but more experienced
Why do you kiss like a porn star?
The question didn't leave her head.
Not that she had ever kissed a porn star, but she imagined that's how they kissed.
Quick tongue chasing and sucking.

She wondered how many girls had gone through his hands
There would be no release for her tonight.
Maybe next time. Instead, she watched the master at work
And hoped he wouldn't notice her watching him.

Broken City

Now you have smeared the whole city with your infidelity.
You have ruined acres of land for me.
Like an airborne disease, it only took a few minutes and the city was ruined,
Tainted by your memories.

Bucharest used to be a city of love, of acceptance,
But not anymore.
Every corner has become a nightmare.
Who knows what's around it?
It's you and your friend, holding hands.

I am glad it happened in your favourite city
Not in mine, Harare. Even your taint can't cross oceans.
I hope it haunts you like it does me.
May the city reject you, spit you out on a pavement
Where you will be licked by stray dogs, with ticks.

The Period

I want to hibernate for a while
So I can wake up and find life enjoyable again.
I want to throw tables and chairs now
And forever when I am angry.
A right only reserved to man.

I want to burn all my friendships
Like how one stubs out a cigarette.
I want to lie on my bed and not feel

Why am I here?
I didn't ask to be born.
I don't want responsibilities, even for my own life
I just want to cry
Nothing is worth living for
Nothing gives me joy
Even fries have lost their taste.

Then like a sledgehammer it hit me
My period is due tomorrow.
Such relief!

Disobedient Poetics—Translating the Third Space: An essay by Tariro Ndoro

[The speech, 'Disobedient Poetics' was first presented at Rutgers University's 'Africa in Translation' Symposium in March 2021 and explores the poetics of Agringada: Like a Gringa, Like a Foreigner.*]*

The story of *Agringada* (Ndoro, 2019) begins in Britain, with the Anglo-Saxons conquering the Welsh, the Irish, and the Scots in the same manner the Romans had conquered them before, it begins with the idea that conquering, ruling, colonising was not simply a political act but a cultural act as well a personal assault in which Welsh and Gaelic became banned languages to allow the proliferation of the Anglo crown culture and the Anglo culture Crown (De Freine, 1978; Jones 2000). Yet this goal of linguistic purity was ironic as the English language itself is a creole of Anglo-Saxon, Latin, Greek and other words of diverse etymology.

The story of what I am arrived on ships in the early 1600s first with the Portuguese who conquered the Mutapas, the proud monarchy that ruled the Zimbabwean plateau at the time (Pikirayi, 2009). There was an exchange of leadership and an exchange of linguistics. Later, in 1816, that same plateau was to be conquered and ruled by the British and it soon became apparent that the only way for Africans to pay the heavy taxes imposed by the colonial government was to work (Pakenham, 1992) and the highest wages that were given to Africans were the ones given to those who were educated both in language and manner i.e. Africans who approximated whiteness.

While Gloria Anzaldua used her theory of borderlands to describe the cultural make-up of the Rio Grande, here I argue that the African continent or at least African linguistics became a borderland at the point of colonisation. Anzaldua defines such borderlands:

> The third world grates against the first and bleeds. And before it forms a scab it hemorrhages again, the lifeblood of two worlds merging to form a third country – a border culture...The new mestiza is a liminal subject who lives in borderlands between cultures races, languages, and genders. As mestizas we are negotiating these worlds every day, understanding that culturalism is a way of seeing an interpreting the world, a methodology of resistance. (Anzaldua, 1990)

In this way colonial and postcolonial subjects are always negotiating with dominant cultures in a struggle that is ongoing. And because the colonial space creates hybrid cultures, the "post-colonial is inherently hybrid" (Buuck, 1997).

The story of what I am does not simply belong to me but to many other black or African writers who felt within their souls a rift, for instance WEB du Bois who described the weight of being Black and American so heavy that it "threatened to rip his soul asunder" (du Bois, 1903). Zimbabwean author, Dambudzo Marechera, for instance, attended a multiracial school at St Augustine's in Penhalonga where most of the texts he read where European, an experience he described as damage done to him by the education system, and a process that was making him a 'nonperson':

> I was being severed from my own voice.... English is my second language, Shona my first. When I talked it was in the form of an interminable argument, one side of which was always expressed English and the other side always in Shona. At the same time would be aware of myself as something indistinct but separate both cultures. (Veit-Wild, 1992)

Theresa Cha describes the similar alienation of one returning from exile in *Dictee*:

> [Then] you return and you are not one of them.... They ask you identity.... Whether or not you are telling the truth or not about your nationality. They say you look other than you are.... You say who you are but you begin to doubt.... Why did you leave this country why are you re- turning? (Cha, 2001)

Achille Mbembe describes postcolonial sensibilities as being "characterized by a distinctive style of political improvisation, by a tendency to excess and lack of proportion, as well as by distinctive ways identities are multiplied, transformed, and put into circulation (Mbembe, 2001) 1. Thus, Marechera's internal conflict resulted in writings (*House of Hunger* (Marechera, 1978), *Black Sunlight* (Marechera, 1988) and *Mindblast* (Marechera, 1984)) that were all disobedient, not only in their linguistics but also in their refusal to pander to nationalist projects. Alice Notley defines the positionality of disobedience as "a refusal of all one should affirm" (Notley, 1998). Marechera first became active whilst living in colonial Rhodesia but through his life also wrote from the positionality of exile and the postcolonial. Buuck notes that in these experiences, Marechera experienced a double alienation and such a "clash of cultural identities and allegiances manifest themselves in a schizophrenic subjectivity that cannot find stable ground within the traditional notions of 'nation,' 'race,' or 'culture'" (Buuck, 1997).

By the time I went to school in the early 1990s the colonial Rhodesia that Marechera was raised in was dead and a new nation called Zimbabwe was born but the money was still in old colonial hands and so my mother, with the great desire to give me advantage, sent me to a multiracial school that would teach me to approximate whiteness so that I would be more employable and that is the story of how I became a cultural chimaera. Like Dambudzo Marechera, I found myself becoming a 'nonperson' by continually bowing down at the altar of conformity and in the words of Marechera, being a "keen accomplice to [my] own mental colonisation" (Veit-Wild, 1997).

Thus, in *Agringada* runs the recurring motif of the horse, that at once represents the proverbial tongue of language and the dressage of Eurocentric education (Ndoro, 2019). Institutions that believed in the breaking of people to make them 'civilised'. In Amiri Baraka's words, I had "[found myself] lost and confused in a land where they wouldn't let [me] speak [my] own oom boom ba boom... [I was] in deep trouble" (Baraka, 1994).

Ironically, Orwell's 1984, although written as a speculation of totalitarianism, can be used to make sense of this denigration of African languages in favour of European ones:

> Newspeak was the official language of Oceania and had been devised to meet the ideological needs of ...English Socialism. The purpose of Newspeak was not only to provide a medium of expression for the world-view and mental habits proper to the devotees of Ingsoc, but to make all other modes of thought impossible. It was intended that when Newspeak had been adopted once and for all and Oldspeak forgotten, a heretical thought.... diverging from the principles of Ingsoc—should be literally unthinkable, at least so far as thought is dependent on words. Newspeak was designed not to extend but to DIMINISH the range of thought...when Oldspeak had been once and for all superseded, the last link with the past would have been severed...In the end we shall make thoughtcrime literally impossible, because there will be no words in which to express it. (Orwell, 1949)

Thus, using European languages as the languages of learning and teaching in postcolonial Africa narrows the African's ability to engage with their own culture. While Amiri Baraka asserts that language is culture, Ngugi Wa Thiong'o elaborates that "as a carrier of culture which embodies ethical and aesthetic values, language constitutes people's perceptions both of themselves their identities, their sense of particularity as members of the human races" (Thiong'o, 1986). Thus, even in postcolonial Africa, suppression of African languages, and the proliferation of European languages distorts the African identities and erases cultural allegiance and memory, disrupting both the inter- and intrapersonal sensibilities of postcolonial subjects, resulting "disassociation of the sensibility of child[ren] from [their] natural and social environment, what we might call colonial alienation." (Thiongo, 1986).

Such alienation, leaves us stranded in cultural borderlands, defined by Anzaldua as, "vague and undetermined place[s] created by the emotional residue of an unnatural boundary" and further argues that such dominant cultures threaten to rename artists or writers if they do not shape themselves. Yet it is imperative that we find our lost voices as Anzaldua points out that ethnicity and language are intricately linked, "I am my language," she says, "Until I can take pride in my language, I can not take pride in myself" (Anzaldua, 1990). Theresa Cha describes the inability to keep one's story, one's language and one's self unacknowledged:

> It murmurs inside. It murmurs. Inside is the pain of speech the pain to say. Larger still. Greater than is the pain not to say. (Cha, 2001)

Anzaldua further points out that women are subjected to a double layer of rigidness as they are oppressed by both patriarchy and the dominant culture (Anzaldua, 1990). Thus, Black women are not only silenced by being separated from African language/culture, but also limited in the arenas they are granted agency. The simplest way to reclaim this culture may seem to be throwing away all things white/European to embrace only what is African. But Flora Veit-Wild expressed the dangers of binaries in the postcolonial positionality as many writers in the immediate post-colonial period were co-opted to write political narratives that only exalted nationalist narratives. She wrote:

> The dichotomies of the anti-colonial era have been replaced by a more complex and multi-layered perception. This perception takes into account the diversities and complexities of African reality in the post-independence era, moving from nation-based anti-colonialism towards a multi-cultural postcolonialism (Veit-Wild, 1997).

Castillo-Garsow argues that where subjects live in such cross-cultural spheres, more multifluous poetics are more effective at representing lived experiences (Castillo-Garsow, 2013). Therefore, Anzaldua advocated for the creation of a third space, a third mindset, a border mentality:

> There, at the juncture of cultures, languages cross-pollinate and are revitalized; they die and are born. Presently this infant language, this bastard language...is not approved by any society. But we ... no longer feel that we need to beg entrance, that we need always to make the first overture—to translate...apology blurting out of our mouths with every step. Today we ask to be met halfway. (Anzaldua, 1990)

In Arthur Rimbaud's words, "A language must be found... This language would be of the soul, for the soul, containing everything, smells, sounds, colours; thought latching on to thought and pulling" (Rimbaud, 1871). Baraka found his African American language by listening to the rhythms of jazz and by honouring the same history that jazz music had done before him (Harris, 2004). Shona writers living in the Rhodesian police state, for instance, would obfuscate their ideals by writing politics in deep Shona. It was in Kwame Dawes' introduction of Tsitsi Jaji's *Carnaval*, in his praise of her shirking this responsibility of being 'THE' African voice (Dawes, 2014) that I realised that the African identity is multi-faceted and its "universal languages" are multifluous. Each African writer can create one's own English (or French or Portuguese or Spanish) to depict one's own history.

The language of each African writer should be particular to their lived experiences as each contemporary writer appropriates English in through their own lens, harking back to the great Chinua Achebe assertion:

> "let no one be fooled though we may write in English we dare to do unspeakable things with it" (Achebe, 1965).

Marechera negotiated his own third space by engaging in syncretism i.e. while English was his dominant language for writing, he subverted it to his own ends:

> One important element of this hybrid situation is the condition of polyglossia. It is through the encounter of two or more languages that the master language, through parody, is decentred, dethroned, debased. (Veit-Wild, 1997)

In her ground-breaking magnum opus, *Dictee* (Cha, 2001), Korean American author Theresa Cha also refused binary classification as only American or only Korean, but created her own third space of exile (Kim, 2013). Her resistance to the dominant culture/language involved using multilingualism as a tool to assert her hybrid identity. Yet it is not only her use of Korean, English, French and Latin that she uses to assert her positionality (Joo and Lux, 2012) but also her calculated use of silence and space to represent trauma (Kim, 2013) and to disrupt and question languages of dominion (Wu, 2004). The late Zimbabwean author, Yvonne Vera uses a similar style of narrative silence represented as mutism in her novel, *The Stone Virgins* to explore trauma and subvert language (Chan, 2005).

In this way, we shake off the "philosophy...of linguistic control and taming the tongue" (Baca, 2008) and embrace a liminal space. Such a liminal space could be subverted for my own purpose by finding a liminal language, thus my take on translating Africa is not in translating pre-existing languages but in finding languages that can translate the lived experience. Lived experiences create lived culture and the space of Shonglish, the inclusion of silences and redactions, the inclusion of Sesotho and Shona and English and Afrikaans in my poetry collection (Ndoro, 2019) is an honest reflection of my borders and my traversing of them: being initiated in a white school as a black girl, existing in a patriarchal world as a woman, negotiating South African existence as a Zimbabwean and bearing witness to two xenophobic uprisings.

The closest I came to *my* personal language was in Safia Elhillo's *January Children* in which she preoccupies herself with the interchange of etymologies (Elhillo, 2017), asking the reader what is lost in translation, what is created, what is preserved. And so, in my writing of *Agringada*, I asserted my own mestiza mentality, first as an entity existing in between English and Shona and then as the product of being a Zimbabwean in non-Zimbabwean spaces. It is not by accident that I chose Spanish etymologies that began first as Latin then evolved into Spanish then clashed with the *lingua francas* of the newly found Americas and finally clashed once more against English to create a different facet of language. It is an English belonging to a particular history and an English that bears witness is not only *legitimate* but necessary. For the word **mustang** to exist, the conquistadors had to have left Spain and the descendants of the first revolutions had to have interfaced with gringos at some stage. The etymology tells the story. This is in line with Nathan Suhr-Sytsma's reading of contemporary African poetics:

> Apart from interlingual intersections and dilemmas, though, twenty-first-century African poets live the necessity of translating between particular experiences, hopes, and insights and more general, often racialized, concepts of Africa. (Suhr-Sytsma, 2019)

Thus, where colonialism sought to limit free thinking by limiting language, today we bear witness by writing, rewriting and reinventing our own Englishes to bear witness to our own unique experiences. In Anzaldua's words, we create "[bridges] by naming ourselves and by telling our stories in our own words" (Anzaldua, 1990).

Bibliography

Achebe, C. (1965). English and the African Author. Transitions 18: 27-30.

Anzaldua, G. (1990). *Borderlands / La Frontera: The New Mestiza*. Aunt Lutte Books.

Buuck, D. (1997). African Doppelganger: Hybridity and Identity in the Work of Dambudzo Marechera. *Research in African Literatures, Summer, 1997, Vol. 28, No. 2, Autobiography and African Literature, 118*-131.

Baca, D. (2008) Mestiza Scripts, Digital Migrations. and the Territories of Writing. New Macmillan.

Baraka, A. (1994). *Wise, Why's, y's: The Griot's Song Djeli Ya*. Third World Press.

Joo, H.S. and Lux, C. (2012) Dismantling Bellicose Idenities: Strategic Language Games in Theresa Hak Kyung Cha's *DICTEE*. *Journal of Transnational American Studies*, 4(1)

Castillo-Garsow, M (2013) The Legacy of Gloria Anzaldúa: Finding a Place for Women of Color in Academia. *Bilingual Review / La Revista Bilingüe*, Vol. 31, No. 1, pp. 3-11

Chan, S. (2005). The memory of violence: Trauma in the writings of Alexander Kanengoni and Yvonne Vera and the idea of unreconciled citizenship in Zimbabwe. *Third World Quarterly*, 26(2), 369–382. https://doi.org/10.1080/0143659042000339164

Dawes, K. (2014). Preface. In *Carnaval* by Tsitsi Jaji (pp. i–iv). Univesity of Nebraska Press.

de Freine, S. (1978). *The Great Silence: The Study of a Relationship Between Language and Nationality*. Irish Books & Media.

du Bois, W. E. B. (1903). *The Souls of Black Folk*. A. C. McClurg & CO.

Elhillo, S. (2017). *The January Children*. University of Nebraska Press.

Harris, W.J. (2004). 'How You Sound??': Amiri Baraka Writes Free Jazz. Uptown Conversation: The new Jazz Studies. Edited by Robert G. O'Meally, Brent Hayes Edwards, and Farah Jasmine Griffin. New York: Columbia University Press. 312-325

Jones, G. E. (2000). The Welsh Language and the Blue Books of 1847. In G. H. Jenkins (Ed.), *The Welsh Language and Its Social Domains* (pp. 431–457). University of Wales Press.

Kim, H.K (2013) Embodying the In-Between: Theresa Hak Kyung Cha's "Dictee". *Mosaic: An Interdisciplinary Critical Journal*, December 2013, Vol. 46, No. 4. 127-143

Marechera, D. (1978). *The House of Hunger*. Heinemman African Writer's Series.

Marechera, D. (1984). *Mindblast*. Heinemman African Writer's Series.

Marechera, D. (1988). *Black Sunlight*. Heinemann (African Writer's Series).

Mbembe, A. (2001). *On the Postcolony*. University of California Press.

Ndoro, T. (2019). *Agringada: Like a Gringa, Like a Foreigner*. Modjaji.

Notley, A. (1998). The Poetics of Disobedience. *The Poetry Foundation*.

Orwell, G. (1949). *Nineteen Eighty-Four*. Secker & Warburg.

Pakenham, T. (1992). Rhodes, Raiders and Rebels. In *The Scramble for Africa* (pp. 497–498). Abacus.

Pikirayi, I. (2009). Palaces, Feiras and Prazos: An Historical Archaeological Perspective of African-Portuguese Contact in Northern Zimbabwe. *The African Archaeological Review, 26*(3), 163–185.

Rimbaud, A. (1871). *A Letter to Georges Izambard*.

Suhr-Sytsma, N. (2019). Theories of African poetry. In *New Literary History* (Vol. 50, Issue 4, pp. 581–607). Johns Hopkins University Press.

Thiong'o, N. (1986). The Language of African Literature. In J. Currey (Ed.), *Decolonising the Mind: The Politics of Language in African Literature.* (pp. 4–33). Oxford University Press.

Veit-Wild, F. (1992). *Dambudzo Marechera: A Source Book on his Life and Work*. Hans Zell.

Veit-Wild, F. (1997). Carnival and hybridity in texts by Dambudzo Marechera and Lesego Rampolokeng. *Journal of Southern African Studies, 23*(4), 553–564.

Wu, C.-Y. (2007). *Language, History and Loss in Theresa Hak Kyung Cha's Dictee*. National University of Taiwan

Acknowledgements

Versions of the following poems have been previously published:

Afric McGlinchey

'Birthstone' was previously published in *Southword*, under the title 'Journey of a Birthstone' (2010)

'White Sky' was published in *New Mirage* (February, 2015)

All Afric's poems appeared in her debut collection, *The lucky star of hidden things*, published by Salmon Poetry in February 2012.

Chioniso Tsikisayi

'I Want to Fall Apart Quietly' in *Brittle Paper* (17 October 2021)

'Planting is a heavy thing' in *Brittle Paper* (24 September 2021)

Marian Christie

'Turbulence' in *The Kent & Sussex Poetry Society Folio 74* (2020)

'Citizen of nowhere' in *The Stony Thursday Book* (Summer 2018)

'And for the rest of time' in *The Fib Review* (#41, Winter 2022)

Samantha Rumbidzai Vazhure

'Travelling by thought' in *Ipikai Poetry Journal* (#4, 2023)

Zahirra Dayal

An extract from 'Where are you really from?' in *Untitled: Voices* (Issue 4, April 2022)

Zaza Muchemwa

'She' was first published on *Badilisha Poetry Xchange* website (2013) and in Zimbabwe Poets for Human Rights poetry anthology *All Protocol Observed* (2013)

Taking flight, winged woman, voluntary voluptuousness

Take flight, winged woman,
raise your arms in a feather bed.
Close your eyes....

Abandon yourself
to a state of voluntary voluptuousness.

Lin Barrie